A Man's Responsibility

ANOTHER JEWISH LIGHTS BOOK
BY RABBI JOSEPH B. MESZLER

Witnesses to the One:
The Spiritual History of the Sh'ma
Foreword by Rabbi Elyse Goldstein

A Man's Responsibility

A Jewish Guide to Being
a **Son**,
a **Partner in Marriage**,
a **Father**,
and a **Community Leader**

Rabbi Joseph B. Meszler

JEWISH LIGHTS Publishing
Woodstock, Vermont

A Man's Responsibility:
A Jewish Guide to Being a Son, a Partner in Marriage, a Father,
  and a Community Leader

2008 Hardcover Edition, First Printing
© 2008 by Joseph B. Meszler

Library of Congress Cataloging-in-Publication Data

Meszler, Joseph B.
  A man's responsibility : a Jewish guide to being a son, a partner in marriage, a father and a community leader / Joseph B. Meszler.
      p. cm.
Includes bibliographical references.
ISBN-13: 978-1-58023-362-0 (hardcover)
ISBN-10: 1-58023-362-7 (hardcover)
1. Jewish men—Religious life. 2. Jewish men—Conduct of life. 3. Masculinity—Religious aspects—Judaism. 4. Sex role—Religious aspects—Judaism. 5. Marriage—Religious aspects—Judaism. I. Title.
BM725.M47 2008
296.7081—dc22

                                                                  2008027548

10   9   8   7   6   5   4   3   2   1

Manufactured in the United States of America
❁ Printed on recycled paper.
Jacket design: Tim Holtz

Published by Jewish Lights Publishing
A Division of Longhill Partners, Inc.
Sunset Farm Offices, Route 4, P.O. Box 237
Woodstock, VT 05091
Tel: (802) 457-4000   Fax: (802) 457-4004
www.jewishlights.com

Contents

Preface   vii

Acknowledgments   xiii

1. Generations   1

2. Beyond Portnoy   11

3. Growing Up and Being a Son   31

4. Growing Up and Being a Partner in Marriage   57

5. Growing Up and Being a Father   91

6. A Man within a Sacred Community   123

7. The *Mitzvot* of Manhood   145

   Notes   159

   Suggestions for Further Reading   169

Preface

In theological exercises with both adolescents and adults, I occasionally ask people to draw God as they pictured God when they were a child. An old man with a white beard, reminiscent of some kind of father or grandfather, is the most popular image. For better or worse, one's definition of God as a child is largely shaped by one's parents, especially one's father. Our culture's patriarchal stereotypes as well as our liturgy present our fathers as a primary likeness of God. This childhood image is invoked throughout our lives as we pray to God to listen to us, to fix our problems, and to pick us up when we have the wind knocked out of us. If we have or had an affectionate father, we often tend to believe in a loving God. If our father was strict, we may believe in a stern God. It is hard to overestimate the impact on our development of *Avinu Malkeinu*, "our Father, our King."

I have been blessed. My father, Richard Meszler, and I are very different in a lot of ways, yet we love each other a great deal. My father is not a religious man, not in the traditional sense. He enjoys the Jewish prayer service when he comes, but he comes only to see me or on some big occasion.

As a rabbi, I believe in communal prayer and a loving God that is the power that makes for peace. My life is filled with Hebrew, Jewish culture, and history. I am privileged to counsel people, give sermons, appear in the media, and write books. My father quietly believes in the laws of nature. He keeps to himself. He is introverted enough that I am sure he is embarrassed reading this paragraph about him by his talkative, extroverted son.

One of my father's greatest gifts to me was to let me pursue a path completely different from his, with his blessing. One day I told him to stop buying me pepperoni because I was keeping kosher. Another time I told him I was going to be a rabbi. "Can you make a living?" he asked. "I think so," I said. No matter how different our choices, we share the duties of providing for and supporting our family.

I am currently watching my father go through a transformation. He has marked it by growing a ponytail. A friend once told me that men do not grow hair casually, although they may claim to do so. It marks a time of transition, of taking on a new face. As my father nears retirement, he will end the years he dedicated to being in a classroom surrounded by students or working quietly in a biological research laboratory. He is preparing to indulge in his more artistic pursuits, including gem cutting and jewelry making. Both his present and future vocations are things I could never do, yet we remain forever connected. I always seek to understand him and his world just as he constantly influences me from the earliest and deepest places in my unconscious.

I have also been privileged to have other male mentors. Mere acknowledgments are completely insufficient and do not do justice to the amount of gratitude I feel toward them, but for the sake of the reader I will be brief. Behind my father was a grandfather, Leo Meszler, who lived a life of kindness. My stepdad, Allan Oshry, is also a kind and compassionate man, and my father-in-law, Jeffrey Zupan, is the definition of graciousness. And I still instinctually call my hometown rabbi, Gustav Buchdahl, whenever I face a new challenge. These men, and others with whom I have also spent time, model the kind of person I would like to be. They have taught me the definition of Jewish men's spirituality.

Jewish Men's Spirituality in Today's World

For centuries, Jewish men have taken on a distinctive role in being responsible before God, their families, and their communities. They understood themselves as keepers of a covenant between

God and the Jewish people, and they knew they were obligated under a code of commandments, *mitzvot*, to fulfill their responsibilities as sons, partners in marriage, fathers, leaders in their community, and other roles. Today, however, this understanding of what constitutes a man's role in society at large seems unclear, and how people define both "Jewish" and "spiritual" is changing. Jewishness is an ambiguous mixture of religion and the residue of ethnicity; spirituality is highly personal and subjective. I understand spirituality to mean the intangible connections that transcend us, including bonds of family, love, duty, and truth, which ultimately lead toward God. Jewish men can see these connections through a specifically Jewish lens, colored by sacred texts and traditions.

I use the term "Jewish men's spirituality" as opposed to "masculinity." Masculinity and femininity are notoriously difficult to define; the matter is not as simple as the stereotypical aggressive versus passive. Indeed, both men and women have traditionally masculine and feminine sides. In speaking of men, therefore, I am speaking of men as complete and whole, as human beings in their entirety.

I believe there is such a thing as Jewish men's spirituality and that it is more necessary than ever. Our world needs wise Jewish men, filled with a sense of purpose, to strengthen our families and our communities.

What I Have Learned

Who are the male mentors in your life whom you aspire to imitate? Who defines the best of being both Jewish and male for you? Perhaps you have yet to meet him.

This book is the product of many meetings with many Jewish men in different synagogues, mostly while serving at Temple Sinai in Sharon, Massachusetts, and Washington Hebrew Congregation in Washington, D.C. These meetings changed how I look at the world and myself. Through making the effort to meet and talk with each other, in the framework of learning about our common Jewish heritage and sharing our experiences, we made time to grow as men.

What I discovered is that, despite the stereotype of men being unwilling to talk about their lives and emotions, there are plenty of things that Jewish men want to talk about, and they are only willing to do so with other men.

The purpose of this book is to explore how a new generation of Jewish men can grow spiritually. It seeks to explain how different generations of Jewish men have had different expectations about work and home, and how the emotional inheritance of one generation is different than the next.

The first two chapters explore in detail the different narratives told by generations of Jewish men in North America to explain themselves. My goal was to unearth some of the male stereotypes that exist in Judaism, coloring our expectations for ourselves and others of what it means to be a Jewish man in today's world. The chapters that follow examine Jewish sources that reveal parts of the life cycle of a man—from son to partner in marriage, to father and member of a community—so as to uncover the ideals that define being a Jewish man.

More could be said about other relationships, such as that of a sibling or a grandfather, but that is beyond the scope of this work. Additionally, I do not presume that all Jewish men have the same sexual orientation or come from similar backgrounds. In striving for transcendent ideals, I seek what it means to be a mature Jewish man and not a boy. The final chapters view the life of a Jewish man in the context of a sacred community.

Finally, while this book can be read in isolation, it is intended to be shared, either by passing it along to a relative or friend or by studying it in a men's group. I have grown by listening to the men around me. In conversation, I have sat with multiple generations and learned from them. I have learned that Jewish men do not fit any stereotype, despite the burdens of past history. I have learned that Jewish sons want desperately to honor their parents and that they struggle if they did not receive the guidance they needed as a child, especially when a father was absent or aloof. I have learned that being a partner in marriage is not simply about being a provider according to the traditional *ketubah* (marriage agreement), but has more to do with partnering to meet individual and mutual needs. I have learned that being a father is the hardest task in the world, where Jewish men struggle not to be pigeonholed into the role of disciplinarian but to be loving and compassionate teachers of wisdom. I have also learned that Jewish men need each other to achieve balance and perspective. I know that to be a Jewish man is ultimately to be responsible, and Jewish tradition can teach me what my responsibilities are.

Following each chapter are questions for reflection. These questions are designed to help the reader more deeply explore issues of Jewish men's spirituality. In addition, groups can use them as a basis for discussion so that Jewish men can learn from one another.

A Note on Translations

For translations of the Hebrew Bible, I have used as my guide the JPS Hebrew-English *Tanakh* (Philadelphia: Jewish Publication Society, 1999) and W. Gunther Plaut and David E. S. Stein, eds., *The Torah: A Modern Commentary*, rev. ed. (New York: Union for Reform Judaism, 2005). Often, I have used the JPS translation and changed references to God so that they are beyond gender. For the sake of consistency, I translate God's Hebrew name as "the Eternal." I have also deviated from these translations when I felt the context called for it. All translations of Rabbinic texts are my own unless otherwise noted. Regularly, I paraphrase texts to make them accessible to a reader new to this literature. Readers are welcome to look up the original passages using the references. In quotations of all other works, I have let masculine-gendered language remain in order to present the authors of such texts with integrity.

Also, I use the word "Torah" not only to refer to the Five Books of Moses but also in the traditional sense of indicating all Jewish wisdom. The word "Israel" refers to the people Israel and not the State of Israel.

Acknowledgments

I would like to begin by thanking the men with whom I have learned for the past eight years in Jewish men's study groups. They are too numerous to mention, but this book is because of them. This is, in fact, *our* book, and many of the men of Temple Sinai in Sharon, Massachusetts, where I serve as rabbi, graciously allowed me to share their stories, although their names have generally been changed, except in cases where someone did not want his identity concealed. I sometimes made composites out of several men's stories for the sake of making a point. Thank you as well to those members of Temple Sinai's men's study group who read the manuscript in advance.

Thanks also go to Dr. Samuel Osherson, Rabbi Stephen Arnold, Rabbi Marcus Burstein, Rabbi Menachem Creditor, Doug Barden, and my sister, Joelle Reizes, for their feedback.

I also need to thank the men in my family previously mentioned in the Preface, even though a simple line of thanks is woefully inadequate: my father, Richard Meszler; my stepfather, Allan Oshry; my father-in-law, Jeffrey Zupan; and my grandfather of blessed memory, Leo Meszler. All have had their imprint on these words.

Similarly, I thank my wife, Rabbi Julie Zupan, for her insight, editing, and love, and my children, Samantha and Justin, who inspired this book. My daily struggle to be the best I can be for them gave birth to the founding of these Jewish men's study groups and this manuscript.

Gratitude also goes to Rabbi M. Bruce Lustig, who sat me down as a newly ordained rabbi and told me of his great idea to start a Jewish men's study group early on Friday mornings and asked if I would lead it. He showed great faith in my abilities.

Finally, I thank Stuart M. Matlins, publisher of Jewish Lights Publishing, who understood the necessity for this book. I would also like to thank Ira Rifkin, a talented editor, who greatly shaped this project. Gratitude also goes to Emily Wichland, Michaela Powell, Debra Corman, and everyone at Jewish Lights who made this happen.

1
Generations

This is the book of the generations of Adam from the day God created human beings, making [them] in the likeness of God, creating them male and female … (Genesis 5:1)

These are the generations of Noah … (Genesis 6:9)

These are the generations of the sons of Noah: Shem, Ham, and Japheth … (Genesis 10:1)

These are the generations of Terah: Terah fathered Abram … (Genesis 11:27)

These are the generations of Isaac, Abraham's son … (Genesis 25:19)

These are the generations of Jacob … (Genesis 37:2)

These are the generations of Aaron and Moses … (Numbers 3:1)

IRV: THE WAY IT WAS

This book is about being a responsible man, a Jew, and a healthy spiritual being. How we understand these aspects of our identity, however, depends greatly on our age because of tremendous generational changes among Jewish men. To grasp this, let's look at the lives of two men, each composite sketches of several men I know, and the world as they see it. We begin with "Irv."

At sixty-four, Irv lives in a suburban community outside of Boston in a comfortable house with a garage and a yard. Irv's wife, Thelma, is responsible for everything that happens inside the house, just as he is responsible for everything outside: the lawn, the trash, and the cars. Irv is nearing retirement from the company where he has worked for over thirty years. His career has been satisfying.

Irv grew up near Blue Hill Avenue, Boston's old Jewish neighborhood, where a simple walk down the street served to remind him of who he was. The G & G Deli was the center of the neighborhood where people met, gossiped, and even ran for elective office. Growing up, Irv attended an Orthodox congregation down the street from his house and became a bar mitzvah, literally meaning "a son of God's commandments," at age thirteen with a coming-of-age ceremony in front of the Torah scroll. His house was kosher; they had separate dishes for milk and meat and did not allow pork or shellfish to enter the kitchen. Outside the house, however, his family was less careful. Irv's mother once said they occasionally would "give God a wink," especially when ordering shrimp in lobster sauce at Chinese restaurants.

Irv's classmates were almost all Jewish, although his teachers weren't. Every winter he endured the annual Christmas assembly where the whole school, led by elderly Irish Catholic teachers, sang Christmas carols. Irv remembers his rabbi telling him and his friends not to worry about this since they were all "good boys."

Just as Irv's school was 99 percent Jewish, the school nearest to his in South Boston was equally Christian. Jews, for the most part, did not venture into this adjacent neighborhood or consider buying a house in that area of the city. Still, there was great ethnic pride in being Jewish. Irv recalls the time a fight with a local Irish gang erupted and why he did not participate. Fighting, his father had told him, is "what the *goyim* do," and never mind the taunt that he was a "sissy." As for his mother, she regarded everyone who was not Jewish as an antisemite. It was a convenient bifurcation of the world.

Irv's father was a bookkeeper and his mother a schoolteacher. This was a great advancement from Irv's immigrant grandparents, who mostly spoke Yiddish and came to America very poor. Whenever he spoke Yiddish to his parents, he was admonished to "speak English!" It was very important to them to fit into this country.

Although Irv grew up in the aftermath of World War II, he was largely unaware of the events of the war and the Holocaust. His parents tried to protect him, and Irv in later years wondered why no one spoke about it back then. On the kitchen table stood a blue and white *pushke*, the Jewish National Fund collection box for the fledgling State of Israel. Irv remembers how his parents took great pride in purchasing trees in Israel to "make the desert bloom."

Irv went to the University of Massachusetts, the first in his family to go to college. While staying in the dormitory, he remembers a swastika being painted on the brick wall near his window. Irv believes this was not personally directed at him but that it was a more general act of antisemitism. For the most part, however, his Jewishness was not an obstacle in his education or his career. Even so, he was aware that some schools and companies were open to Jews and that others simply were not. Irv went on to earn a master's degree at Northeastern University and then found a job working on computer systems for the government. His daily commute was a little over a half hour. Like clockwork, he left home at eight and returned a little after six. He worked hard, and his life followed an ordered pattern.

Irv and Thelma married when he was still an undergraduate. They were set up by a mutual friend, a date that Irv agreed to reluctantly. They were both twenty-two years old at the time, but by age thirty they were married with four children. Rather than live in the old neighborhood, they moved farther out into the suburbs. By doing so, they barely missed the blockbusting that took place in Boston when banks and real estate agents gave mortgages and sold houses to African Americans in Jewish neighborhoods in a successful attempt to panic Jews into selling their homes before they found themselves stranded in a changed neighborhood. A great deal of money was made by these agents as Jews sold their houses for under market value and these same houses were then sold to African American families at exorbitant prices.

Israel's victory in the 1967 Six-Day War evoked great pride among American Jews, and it was no different for Irv. He remembers that time with great fondness. "We won!" he thought, though today he is unsure if political correctness allows him to express that sort of tribal glee. Although his parents taught him that Jews did not physically fight their enemies but instead overcame adversaries by pursuing an education and leading successful lives, Irv couldn't help but feel good over a Jewish army winning a war so decisively.

Thelma worked out of the house as soon as all of the children were of school age, but only during school hours. She went to work full-time only after the children graduated from high school. Child rearing and household chores were her primary responsibilities. It helped that Thelma is a very good cook. Today, both Irv and Thelma are deeply satisfied with their home life together and their relationship roles. Irv takes care of the finances. He feels a deep sense of responsibility for his family, and he considers providing for his loved ones "a man's work."

Irv and Thelma joined a Conservative synagogue and sent their children to its Hebrew school in the afternoons and on Sunday morning. They have stayed loyal members for many years. Many of their friends belong to the same synagogue, and it is the center of their social circle. Irv enjoys schmoozing with his friends at the *oneg*, or dessert, after the service. All of his children became bar and bat mitzvah there. He especially remembers with pleasure his daughter singing in the children's choir.

Years later, two of his children married Jewish partners, and two did not. Of the mixed couples, one decided to raise their children as Jews, but the other has not. Irv feels a great deal of anxiety over how to be a grandfather to his non-Jewish grandchildren. He accepts that his children are free to make their own choices, but when he sees these grandchildren around the Christmas tree, he sometimes feels he has failed. He cannot help but give them Chanukah presents wrapped in gift-wrap decorated with menorahs to remind them of their Jewish heritage.

When Irv looks at the next generation, he knows that times have changed. Life seems so much more complicated for them. The range of choices today seems confusing, and expectations have become unclear. Nevertheless, he firmly believes that life is what you make of it and that no one has ever had it easy.

Recently, Irv overheard a man with a strong Yiddish accent speaking to a supermarket cashier. The sound of his voice brought back memories of Irv's childhood, and a wonderful feeling came over him. It occurred to him that his children missed something by not hearing that sound in their everyday life.

BRIAN: THE WAY IT IS NOW

"I leave when it's dark and come home when it's dark, and the first thing I do when I get home is change a diaper," says a Jewish man I'll call Brian, a thirty-nine-year-old father of two. Brian is a doctor, as is his wife, Claire. They recently purchased a large house in the western suburbs of Boston with an equally large mortgage. The house has big bedrooms with plenty of play space for their children. Wide windows let in a great deal of sunlight. The landscaping around the house is professionally done and maintained. Cleaners are hired to come to their home once every two weeks. They also hired a nanny to help with childcare. With both of them working, such hired help is a necessity. Brian puts in the ridiculous office hours that most physicians keep, and Claire works part-time in an emergency room.

Brian met Claire when they were in medical school. They began studying together and were immediately attracted to each other, but both wanted to finish their education before marrying. However, Claire was not Jewish, and that made Brian uncomfortable. They even broke up for a short while over it. But after dating others, Brian realized there was no one else he wanted to be with. He was deeply in love.

Today, Brian's parents are embarrassed to say they were not especially gracious when Brian and Claire announced their engagement. The Jewish family they had always envisioned sitting around the Passover Seder table or lighting Chanukah candles seemed jeopardized. Would their grandchildren learn about Jesus and have a Christmas tree? In many ways, they, like Irv, felt they had failed.

The more they got to know Claire, however, the more they realized it was impossible not to love her. Claire is a beautiful person, inside and out. She happily learned to make kugel and brisket. Brian and Claire were married by a justice of the peace in a ceremony that contained Jewish symbols; they had a *chuppah*, or wedding canopy, and Brian stomped on a glass at the end. To Brian's great relief, Claire readily agreed to raise their children as Jews, since she lacked a strong connection to her Christian upbringing. Even though Brian is anything but a regular at synagogue services, he feels responsible for passing Judaism on to his children. Anything else would leave him feeling he was letting down the countless generations of Jews who preceded him—not the least of which are his parents.

Brian and Claire now have two girls. Both being doctors, they badgered their obstetrician with unending questions and suggestions, and Brian was there at both births, coaching Claire all the way. He also reflects upon how much times have changed: "When Claire was born, she tells me that her father actually went out fishing! He was not expected to be anywhere near the hospital."

Still, Brian relies heavily on Claire for raising their children, although he is in no way an absentee dad. He tries when he can to attend important events in his daughters' lives, such as dance recitals, and each Sunday he likes to play with both girls at the local indoor pool. He hopes to coach a sport they might play when they are older, perhaps soccer or softball. He realizes, however, that his workdays often fly by and that he is often late getting home. His work seems endless, but he cares a great deal about his patients and is committed to them.

When it came time to enroll their eldest child in preschool, Brian and Claire turned to their local synagogue. The Jewish pre-school intrigued Claire. She grew up with many Jewish friends, and of course, she married a Jew. As she became increasingly involved in preschool activities, she began to feel that something was missing in her life—a sense of connectedness and belonging. After a thoughtful and deeply personal process, she decided to convert to Judaism. She began taking classes and before she knew it, she was the family's "Jewish expert," a common occurrence in intermarried families where the Jewish spouse is only marginally familiar with Jewish religious and cultural traditions.

It was thrilling and deeply moving for Brian to see Claire discover Judaism on her own. Brian has always been proud of being Jewish and remembers his bar mitzvah as a great day. He also remembers it as his "get out of jail free card," for he never went back to Hebrew school after that and his family attended services only on Rosh Hashanah and Yom Kippur. Above all, he did not want to push Claire into anything; it was important to him that she knew he loved her for exactly who she was.

Still, he was amazed at how energized she became about being Jewish. She gave him books to read that she had used to study for her conversion. She instigated lighting Shabbat candles on Friday night, having a Shabbat dinner, and on occasion taking the girls to synagogue "Tot Shabbat" services. He thinks it's great she is so into Jewish life and ritual, as he sees himself as too busy for that part of life. At the same time, he feels a bit guilty he is not more involved, since it is his religion that Claire adopted. He knows he is supposed to be more active, but in truth he doesn't even know the names of his daughters' Hebrew school teachers.

Each year, Passover Seder takes place at Brian's parents' house, and Claire's parents come as well. Where previously they raced through the Haggadah in fifteen minutes or so to get to the matzah ball soup, Claire now likes to slow things down; she asks questions and says a prayer for their whole family. Everyone appreciates how Claire has added a spiritual dimension to the ceremony. Brian's father is in charge of hiding the *afikoman*, and he always brings up the subject of the State of Israel, especially because the last words of the Haggadah are "Next year in Jerusalem!" It occurs to Brian that this is really the only time that they ever have this kind of conversation.

Brian remembers his own Hebrew school experience. Despite the complaints he and his peers raised about the additional late-afternoon studying, they actually had a good time. Holidays were celebrated with special foods, and he remembers one teacher who told fantastic stories. Simchat Torah was especially fun, marching with a miniature Torah scroll, waving an Israeli flag, and eating an entire chocolate bar. Brian's Hebrew reading skills are not as good as they once were, but he still feels a draw to the synagogue to mark important milestones: a family wedding, the funeral for the father of a friend, and the naming of his children.

Even so, if it weren't for Claire, he might not go at all. Brian isn't sure if there is much there for him. Once he went to a Hebrew school family education program with his daughters, and it seemed he was intruding on a "Moms' Club" meeting. There were only two other men, and he joined them standing in the corner, drinking coffee. When they sat down for the activity, he felt kind of foolish using fabric scissors and gluing felt for an arts and crafts project. He was anxious to go home to watch the football game on television that afternoon.

BEING JEWISH AND MALE IN THE TWENTY-FIRST CENTURY

A new generation of Jewish men is seeking an understanding of its obligations as sons, partners in marriage, and fathers. But to do so, it is necessary to first understand the preceding generation and its assumptions because so much of how we understand our lives is handed down from generation to generation. To know who we are requires knowing where we come from. We learn about ourselves by comparing and contrasting the historical narratives that we tell.

Irv's Jewish identity and spiritual resources derive largely from his ethnicity as a Jew. He absorbed his feeling of connectedness from the accents, smells, and sensations around him. In the time of his childhood, white ethnic groups remained largely segregated by neighborhood. Additionally, he and his wife adhere to sharply defined relationship boundaries. The parameters of his familial role are just as clear to him as the expectation that he would be home by a certain time for dinner and that a meal cooked by his wife awaited him. Irv's anxiety comes partially from feeling that those parameters and his world are fading from existence.

In contrast, Brian's world, both within the larger society and within Judaism, has blurred boundaries. Ethnic ties are almost completely absent—traded, it seems, for feelings of empowerment and freedom, but also stress. He waited until he completed his education to marry, and has fewer children. Judaism has its time and place as an extracurricular activity but must compete for a slot on his hand-held electronic calendar device.

I am a rabbi and a Jewish professional, but I still count myself as a part of this new generation in that I am personally in search of what it means to be Jewish and a man today, especially in comparison with Jewish men my father's age. I therefore include myself among this younger group with the occasional use of the pronoun "we."

In the next chapter, I'll address in greater detail how these generational changes have left the contemporary American Jewish male adrift and the implications this has for Jewish life—in the home, in the synagogue, and for the Jewish and non-Jewish communities. I'll also start to consider what is required for the American Jewish man to change course for the benefit of his loved ones, society, and—just as importantly—himself.

QUESTIONS FOR REFLECTION

- To which generation do you belong, Irv's or Brian's?

- If you belong to Irv's generation, did you grow up in a Jewish neighborhood like his? Do you have similar memories of the Six-Day War or the Yom Kippur War? How do you feel when you hear a Yiddish accent?

- If you belong to Brian's generation, do you live in a suburban neighborhood like his? Do you work as many hours as he does? How do you balance your time?

- What are the differences between Irv and Brian? What are the similarities?

- How do Irv and Brian each express their Jewish identities?

- Do you have interfaith relationships/marriages in your family?

- How do you and family members feel about them?

- How do you feel when you enter a synagogue? Comfortable or uncomfortable? Do you belong to a synagogue? Why or why not?

- As seen in the opening quotation, the Torah keeps track of time by listing generations. Do you relate to this sense of generational connection?

2

Beyond Portnoy

While the pressures connected to trying to be a responsible man are hardly new, in the past few decades there have been tremendous changes in the world of the average Jewish male. Internal and external forces have created a situation in which there is a gap between fathers and sons, between one generation and another. How younger men work, play, and pray is different than how their fathers did.

The majority of younger Jewish men today are better educated than their fathers, but they also work longer hours and have longer commutes. According to the 2000–2001 National Jewish Population Survey, 61 percent of Jewish men today have a college degree, and an astounding 29 percent hold a graduate degree. (The comparable figures for the total U.S. population are 29 percent and 6 percent, respectively.)[1] Advanced education has not meant fewer hours at work. At the start of the twentieth century the number of men working fifty hours or more was declining. But since 1970 the trend has been an increase in hours for better compensation. This trend applies especially to men with a higher education, of which Jewish men are disproportionately represented.

Even with the feminist revolution, men still generally work longer hours than women do and therefore have less time away from their careers. The U. S. Department of Labor reports that out of the total population in 2005, about 60 percent of women were part of the work force, compared to approximately 75 percent of men.[2] Of these workers, women were far more likely to work part-time than men, 86 percent of whom worked at least forty hours a week.[3] The number of hours in the workweek for everyone has also steadily climbed, with an overall increase of 14.4 percent among top wage earners since the 1970s.[4] In addition, according to the United States 2000 Census, the number of commuters traveling ninety minutes or more to and from work has doubled in the last decade alone. Increasing numbers begin their commute earlier in the day, many as early as 5 a.m.[5]

Inside the family, many men have a different understanding of the demands of marriage and parenting than did their fathers. Men today often seek to share child rearing and other household duties with their spouses instead of restricting themselves to the defined role of breadwinner. Believing in gender equality, more women work out of the house by choice, even when the children are young. In the name of liberation, men and women have refused to define themselves by what they view as constricting roles, sharing instead the joys and challenges of work and family.

However, the sacrifices are tremendous. By doing more at home, men never go "off duty."[6] Younger men work at work and work at home. They have little time to be alone (outside of commuting time in a car) or at leisure. What may be liberating psychologically is binding in terms of physical time and space.

Unfortunately, just because men take on more household chores and parenting responsibilities does not mean they give up believing they should also be the family's main provider. Men, in fact, want greater work-hour flexibility to meet these new demands at home but not necessarily shorter hours.[7]

All this means that men today are more stressed and have less time than a generation ago. Jewish men as educated, high-wage earners model this fact in the extreme. As Jewish men become more assimilated, religious pursuits become a casualty of these lifestyle changes and time constraints. Whereas the synagogue was once dominated by men, men are now increasingly absent from synagogue life. Doug Barden, executive director of Men of Reform Judaism (formerly the North American Federation of Temple Brotherhoods), describes it as "male flight" from liberal synagogue life.[8] (By "liberal," I mean to generally include Reform, Reconstructionist, and some Conservative and nondenominational synagogues that explicitly promote egalitarianism. In a traditional synagogue, a sense of obligation, "commandment," and conventional gender roles still hold greater sway, as does patriarchal authority.)

In the liberal synagogue, men today are not as often found at committee meetings or working as teachers in the religious school. They do not attend services or adult education programs in the same numbers as women. Some speak of a general 70:30 female-to-male ratio and, in some congregations, even 80:20.[9] Men are too busy sitting in the car for long hours to and from work and changing diapers at home (two things their fathers probably did not do) to find time to pray or study.

But being busy does not solely explain the absence of men from liberal synagogue life. After all, even though men are generally more obsessed with their work than are women, plenty of working women still make time for the synagogue. Some additional reasons for men's absence come from embarrassment at their ignorance of Judaism and feeling they are not required for the synagogue to function, for women seem to be "running the show."

Many men feel a special pride in appearing competent. In fact, research has shown that high testosterone levels usually manifest themselves in attempts to demonstrate dominance, not in acts of aggression.[10] For the high-testosterone male, appearing incompetent feels shameful. Jewish men, especially, seem to resist registering for synagogue classes labeled "introductory" or "basic" and often feel humiliated by their inability to read Hebrew aloud during public worship.

In addition, the synagogue itself has changed. A generation ago, Jewish men looked to the synagogue for support in navigating life's challenges. They were part of a *minyan* (a prayer quorum) or an auxiliary group, such as the synagogue men's association, upon which they could lean for support. In doing so, they identified themselves as Jews and were there for each other during life's sorrows and joys.

Today's generation has a much more ambivalent relationship to the synagogue and its associations. The synagogue no longer seems to need men to function. Men are no longer required to complete a *minyan* at Reform, Reconstructionist, and most Conservative synagogues (the majority of synagogues in North America), for women are now counted. Feminism has empowered women to take on greater roles in synagogue life, including as clergy and presidents of boards. It is therefore tempting to let women take care of the religious sphere of life. When we receive a call from the synagogue about a social action volunteer project, an adult education class, or how a child is doing in religious school, it is very easy to say, "Speak to my wife."[11]

The new generation of Jewish men does not involve itself in liberal synagogue life to the same degree for these reasons and more. One can either feel relaxed and competent on the golf course or embarrassed and unnecessary at *shul.* Simply put, most Jewish men today would rather spend their prized Saturday morning hours in the center of a field coaching their daughters at soccer than sitting off to the side in a sanctuary, stammering and trying to follow a prayer service.

The Burden of History

What we may not realize is that in each generation our world is shaped by forces beyond our control. These forces can be seen in the cultural products of the past hundred years. Looking at them we can see that Irv's and Brian's assumptions and choices did not occur in a vacuum. Powerful forces of ethnicity, antisemitism, and Zionism shaped the identity of Irv's generation of Jewish men in North America. These factors are considerably less influential today.

In Philip Roth's famous novel *Portnoy's Complaint*, published in 1969, the narrator travels to Israel two years after the Six-Day War. Looking out an airplane window at Tel Aviv below, he reminisces about growing up watching the men on the softball field near his house. The two images, he knows, are related—that of the muscular, sweaty men throwing a ball and the robust Jewish state. Being a "nice Jewish boy" and a "Diaspora Jew," he feels shame as he touches down. He realizes that the main reason he is traveling to Israel is "to watch the men."

> And that's the phrase that does me in as we touch down upon *Eretz Yisroel*: to watch the men. Because I love those men! I want to grow up to *be* one of those men!... I should stay. Yes, stay! Buy a pair of those khaki short pants—become a man![12]

Philip Roth's character is a caricature of what it felt like to be a Jewish man during the late twentieth century in North America. His portrait is an extreme; the narrator confesses to being effeminate, unable to escape his mother, sexually perverted and frequently impotent, and constantly whining and complaining. This stereotype is not new. Roth brought to the foreground an image that had existed for centuries; the representation of the effeminate Jewish male pervaded literature about Jews for hundreds of years. Jewish men are paradoxically portrayed as feminine and feeble and at the same time lecherous and malicious by writers as famous as Shakespeare, Milton, and Eliot.[13]

Given this cultural inheritance, many Jewish men lived with the assumption that Jewish men—including themselves—were "sissies." Jewish men were perceived as bookish and weak. They could not fight to defend themselves or work jobs that required physical labor. (A friend of mine who attended a performance by the comedian Jackie Mason told me Mason made everyone laugh with two words: Jewish farmer.) Overly intellectual, Jewish men were thought incapable of knowing the right end of a power tool (or a gun) if their lives depended upon it. They lost their machismo sometime back in the days of the Maccabees. As a minority spread across many lands, Jews were considered uprooted and sapped of strength. Sigmund Freud claimed that circumcision was a symbolic substitute for castration,[14] and some Christian polemicists even believed Jewish men menstruated.[15]

Freud, in fact, recorded this now famous passage about a walk with his father:

> I may have been ten or twelve years old when my father began to take me with him on his walks and reveal to me in his talk his views upon things in the world we live in. Thus it was, on one such occasion, that he told me a story to show me how much better things were now than they had been in his days. "When I was a young man," he said, "I went for a walk one Saturday in the streets of your birthplace; I was well dressed, and had a new fur cap on my head. A Christian came up to me and with a single blow knocked off my cap into the mud and shouted: 'Jew! Get off the pavement!'" "And what did you do?" I asked. "I went into the roadway and picked up my cap," was his quiet reply. This struck me as unheroic conduct on the part of the big, strong man who was holding the little boy by the hand.[16]

Freud's description is ominous for us today. His father claims life is better than it was, but Freud lived before the Shoah (Hebrew for the Holocaust). With the pain of hindsight, we know that life was not as Freud's father saw it, but was, in fact, about to become far worse than he could ever imagine. The "unheroic conduct"[17] of his father fills the young Freud with shame. The agenda of antisemites was to denigrate Jews for economic and political gain, and humiliating Jewish men was a method of disempowering them.

This antisemitic agenda came to a head with two epoch-making events in the history of Judaism, the Shoah and the founding of the

State of Israel. The words of the Austrian philosopher Otto Weininger epitomize the kind of rhetoric the Nazis used:

> Judaism is saturated with femininity, with precisely those qualities the essence of which I have shown to be in the strongest opposition to male nature. It would not be too difficult to make a case for the view that the Jew is more saturated with femininity than the Aryan, to such an extent that the most manly Jew is more feminine than the least manly Aryan.[18]

In this way, the Nazis depicted the "manly Aryan" against the effeminate yeshiva student. In this atmosphere, what Jewish boy could possibly want to identify as a religious Jewish male?

From Antisemitism to Zionist Propaganda

Combining misogyny and antisemitism, haters of the Jewish people sought to define Jewish men as effete and therefore weak and disgusting.[19] Unfortunately, many Jewish men internalized these antisemitic motifs. Bombarded with messages of their so-called pathetic frailty, some Jews furthered these stereotypes themselves. Consider the words of "Jewish self-hatred" by the German Jewish philosopher Theodor Lessing from 1930:

> Do you know how it feels to curse the soil on which one lives? To draw poison from one's roots instead of nourishment? Do you know what it means to be ill-born, begotten in the nuptial bed of calculation and superficial selfishness? To be ill-protected, neglected, pampered, effeminate and thrashed?[20]

The Hebrew poet Haim Nahman Bialik similarly criticized Jews for their cowardice during the Kishinev pogrom, arguing that they died in an unmanly fashion when attacked by mobs. His words record his disgust:

> Come, now, and I will bring thee to their lairs
> The privies, jakes, and pigpens where the heirs
> Of Hasmoneans lay, with trembling knees,
> Concealed and cowering,—the sons of the Maccabees![21]

It is instructive that both of the previous quotations came from Zionists (advocates for the establishment of the State of Israel). The antisemitic stereotype of the Jewish male as wimp answered for some Jews the question as to why the Jewish people did not fight back with arms against their oppressors. (In fact, many did fight back during the Shoah; the Warsaw Ghetto uprising and the escape from the concentration camp Sobibor are the most prominent examples of this truth.) The myth of Jewish weakness in other lands became central to Israeli identity for Zionists trying to convince Jews to leave the Diaspora for Israel. In the Diaspora, it was understood, Jews could not defend themselves. Only by working Jewish soil in a Jewish state backed by a Jewish army could one truly be a Jewish man.

Being a Jewish man in North America a generation ago, as defined by antisemites and by Zionists, meant being weak and effeminate. For antisemites, this was a belief born out of hate. For Zionists, it was part of the self-definition of the State of Israel. Jewish men were supposed to be dependent upon Israel for their masculinity, to feel macho. It meant moving to the State of Israel to avoid being a wimp. The twentieth-century myth of Jewish manhood was about trying to survive a gentile world with one's pride intact. Rabbi Jeffrey Salkin, in *Searching for My Brothers: Jewish Men in a Gentile World,* recalls the pride he felt after the Israeli victory in 1967 when a Catholic schoolmate said to him, "Hey, you guys can really fight!"[22] For Salkin, Israel restored Jewish "manhood," a "masculine fantasy" come true:

Centuries of passivity came to an end in May 1948, when the State of Israel was born. Never again would Jews have to sketch maps to scoot through the neighborhoods of the world, fearing both the blows of the anti-Semitic bullies and the laughter of apathetic neighbors. It was as if a body-building manual had arrived at our doorsteps.[23]

Jacob and Esau

Within traditional Judaism, some have illustrated Jewish masculinity through the biblical example of the twin brothers Jacob and Esau. The book of Genesis tells us: "When the boys grew up, Esau became a skillful hunter, a man of the outdoors; Jacob was a mild man who stayed in camp" (Genesis 25:27).

In the Torah's narrative, Esau is the firstborn, and he is favored by his father. In addition, Esau is described as being hairy all over, like an animal. He likes to hunt and kill things. In later Jewish writing, the fierce Esau is rejected in sacred literature as a gluttonous idolater.[24] The Jewish Sages of antiquity, in fact, used the name Esau as a code word for the Romans, whom they despised.[25]

Jacob, on the other hand, is smooth-skinned, intelligent, and his mother's favorite. Jacob becomes a patriarch of the Jewish people by deceiving his father through a clever ruse instigated by his mother. Despite this questionable use of his talents, Jacob wins the right to be leader of the tribe. He is praised by the Rabbis for renewing the covenant with God and passing it on to his children and grandchildren.[26]

Modern commentators, however, informed by centuries of Jewish male stereotyping, have reread the Jacob and Esau narrative and added a new interpretation. Some see in Jacob a figure less manly than his brother. His mother is said to have "dominated" him, and Jacob is "filled with fear."[27] In other words, he is not just "mild" but a mama's boy. Salkin writes that Jacob's wrestling (and overpowering) an angel in Genesis 32:25–33 is actually not an example of Jacob's will and strength. Rather, in that episode, Jacob's leg is wrenched at the hip, and this is seen as a wound "in his groin, in his masculinity."[28]

Real Jewish Men

Salkin writes that being an authentic Jewish man is about "Torah rather than toughness."[29] I would disagree, somewhat, by emphasizing that such a characterization is still a stereotype. In reality, the idea that Jewish men are not tough is simply untrue. Jewish men are by no means lacking in strength.[30] We need only reflect briefly to realize there is plenty of evidence of Jewish machismo, both for good and for bad.

Jews have served with distinction in the armed forces of many countries in which they were citizens, as the Jewish War Veterans of the United States, Jewish War Veterans of Canada, and the histories of Great Britain, Germany, France, Italy, and other countries proudly attest.

Jews have excelled in sports, from Hank Greenberg and Sandy Koufax, to Mark Spitz and Ike Berger (who set twenty-three world and Olympic weightlifting records, won a gold medal at the 1956 Melbourne Olympics, and is a cantor to boot).

Jews even have their own history of thugs, including the organized crime bosses Meyer Lansky and Ben "Bugsy" Siegel, who promoted the development of Las Vegas.[31]

The truth is that real Jewish men are men who do not fit any stereotype. Today, there are macho Jewish men and effeminate Jewish men, intellectual Jewish men and uneducated Jewish men, physically strong Jewish men and physically weak Jewish men. In short, Jewish men come in every imaginable type—just like men in every other ethnic, racial, or religious grouping. It's important to distinguish carefully between reality and stereotypes created to serve an agenda. Just as it is wrong to define femininity as passive, so it is incorrect to say that masculinity, Jewish masculinity included, is solely an issue of strength. Symbols and narratives are extremely important but need to be understood for what they are—not necessarily factual.

The Blessings and Curses of Assimilation

Forty years have passed since the Six-Day War when Israel galvanized the Jewish world with its victory. For Jewish men who remember those years, many of the stereotypes about Jewish men taken for granted back then remain very powerful. For Jewish men born later, for whom the State of Israel has always been a military juggernaut, who have not experienced antisemitism in their schools or organizations, and who have no firsthand recollection of Yiddish-speaking grandparents, masculinity is not defined by antisemitic images or Zionist mythology. Acceptance by the surrounding culture has distanced the younger generation from these forces. While the residue of antisemitism, as well as the occasional encounter, may still impact them, their Jewish identity is based less on how others may perceive them and more on their individual choices.

The downside is that as Jews have gained greater security they have also tended to assimilate more. The feeling of confidence and the desire to fully enter into society go hand in hand. As Jews living in the Diaspora gain equality in their adopted nations they identify less as ethnic Jews and more as Americans, Canadians, or whatever their nationality may be. Being Jewish is no longer the obstacle it once was to getting a job or being included, and Jewish men on the whole do not see being Jewish as a liability. It is simply a fact of life, and for many not a particularly important one. We are no longer embarrassed about being Jewish, but we're not necessarily excited about it either. Being Jewish is just another part of one's life, equal if not less important than one's profession or even one's hobbies.

Such changes impact greatly how many see themselves as Jews and as men. In addition, the Jewish family has changed into a mixed multitude of ethnicities and backgrounds, with interfaith families, interracial families, gay and lesbian families, and single-parent families, as well as traditional families of multiple generations. Rather than seeing ourselves as fighting against gentiles, we are more likely today to marry them. The rate of intermarriage for couples before 1970 was 13 percent. From 1996 to 2001 it was 47 percent.[32]

There is a blessing and a curse to such assimilation. The reward of achieving the American dream is safety and social success. Openness also brings blessings of inclusiveness and tolerance. The danger is losing our values in a consumer-based, fast-paced, materialistic, fantasy-driven society. In North America, nonacceptance is no longer the threat; today the threat to a vibrant Jewish future is ambivalence about being Jewish.

Here's the challenge: Will you let the values of the surrounding culture completely define who you are, or will you look to your heritage to define yourself? *Can you as a contemporary Jewish man find the required resources within the wellspring of Jewish tradition to be the kind of man you want to be even while being a part of a blended society?*

The Hardest Time of Day

My own experience is not much different than that of other contemporary husbands and fathers. I usually start my workday at 8:30 in the morning. I work very hard at dealing with the joys and challenges of being the sole rabbi of a congregation. One must deal with the expectations and anxieties, both reasonable and unreasonable, of a large group of people.

I love what I do, but that does not mean it is without stress. The stress of my job is not much different than the stress in other occupations. Whether one works in business or industry, provides health care, or offers other types of professional services, all occupations are ultimately people oriented. My vocation is a privilege, but working with people is never simple.

Neither is living with them.

Being a rabbi is easy compared to being a husband and father. I come home after my last appointment of the afternoon to eat dinner, help our children with bath time, and get them ready for bed. Then I usually need to turn around and go back to the temple for a meeting or some other evening event. When I arrive home for dinner my wife is waiting for me. She cannot wait for me to come home because she needs a break. I know she often wants to say, "It's your turn." She has been with the children all day, schlepped baskets of laundry up and down the stairs several times and, in between, scrambled to squeeze in some preparation for classes she teaches on several weekday evenings.

When I arrive, our children greet me with excitement, and there is no better feeling in the world than being hugged tightly by their little arms. These hugs mark my transition from rabbi to dad. The children want and need my attention. I immerse myself in the thick of it all. I mediate when the children both want the same toy that, for some reason, is the only one that will satisfy them at that moment, despite the hundreds of other toys available to them. They also mysteriously need to play in the exact same three square feet of floor space. Displaced puzzle pieces litter the floor along with battery-powered plastic play things that make constant noise. I love my children with all the joy in the world, yet given enough willful hysterics on their part, and sleep deprivation on mine, I find my patience quickly wearing very thin. Of course, this is my wife's life while I am at work. While this is going on, I try to collaborate with my wife on the dinner that is being quickly prepared in the kitchen. Baths, stories, and bedtime are fast approaching, and I need to get to that evening meeting.

During this chaos the phone inevitably rings, heralding either a phone solicitation or someone who just wants to ask something quick: "I promise it won't take a minute." The implication is: won't you please give me your undivided attention right now?

I must admit there are times when I disappear into the bathroom to steal a few minutes of quiet. Here I am, respected in my job, a supposed authority in my community, and knowledgeable in Jewish sacred writings and wisdom, hiding behind a closed door, sitting on the toilet, reminiscent of what one did to escape bullies in elementary school.

I think back to how it was supposed to have been for the previous generation of men, to how Irv must have felt. I can picture him now: He walks in the front door and is greeted lovingly. One of his kids brings him the paper while another takes his coat. He sits in the living room, Scotch in hand, shoes off, feet up, while his wife tells the children to quiet down, "your father has had a hard day." She has spent a good part of the afternoon preparing a delicious meal, while the angelic kids, who all somehow reflect the patriarch's good looks, sit and do their homework. The hero during the day is equally revered at home.

Yes, yes, I know it was never really this way. How many of our fathers came home and, before even saying hello, poured themselves a drink? How many were quiet but tense? Did we notice that too often their silence hid a sense of being overwhelmed within the four walls of their own domicile?

Many men view the return to home as a gain of family time but as also a loss. We go from being the powerful authority at work to being the frustrated and harassed parent and husband who needs to help get dinner on the table if he wants to eat and get his children's clothes off their bodies if he wants them clean. Walking in the front door, therefore, means not only hugs and kisses but also surrendering power and certainty. It may feel easier to work long hours in the office, where one's role is clear, than to navigate the mysterious universe called home. I suspect many men unconsciously stay late at work to hang on to their feeling of competence as along as possible.

Dr. Samuel Osherson, a leading expert on male psychology, calls the late afternoon–early evening period "potentially explosive" for modern families. It is a transitional time, a time when husband and wife "need to validate that both are needy, that both person's daily experiences are worthwhile, and that no one will have his or her needs met entirely."[33] The emotional effort required to accomplish this realization in the heat of the moment is enormous.

"God's Loneliest Creature?"

The problem of being a good family man while also working hard is an ancient one in Judaism. Consider that the Torah indicates that even Moses struggled with this balance. The book of Exodus records the moment when Moses comes home from "work," work that no one can dispute was worthwhile. The story recounts how Moses faces Pharaoh, brings God's ten plagues down upon on Egypt, and leads his people out of slavery. He raises his staff to part the Sea of Reeds and leads his people to the other side. He satisfies thirsty Israelites in search of water with miracles and defends them against hostile tribes. Moses, so to speak, has a full day at the office.

The Torah then tells us that Moses's father-in-law, Jethro, has been watching over Moses's wife and two sons this whole time. One has to wonder what a father-in-law thinks of his married daughter and two grandchildren returning to his home while his son-in-law is off gallivanting around obeying the voice of God. Jethro finds Moses leading the Israelites through the wilderness:

> Jethro, Moses's father-in-law, took Zipporah, Moses's wife, after she had been sent home, and her two sons.... Jethro, Moses's father-in-law, brought Moses's sons and wife to him in the wilderness, where he was encamped at the mountain of God. He sent word to Moses, "I, your father-in-law Jethro, am coming to you, with your wife and her two sons." Moses went out to meet his father-in-law; he bowed low and kissed him; each asked after the other's welfare, and they went into the tent. (Exodus 18:2–7)

The Hebrew Bible employs a style of emphasis through repetition. In this small section alone, the Torah goes out of its way to repeat that Jethro was Moses's father-in-law four times and that he was bringing Moses's wife and sons three times. Can we read some tension in these relationships that Moses has neglected while he was off saving the Israelites? Consider also that the Bible usually leaves out details like time, place, or any chitchat. And yet we are told that these two men greeted each other, asked how the other was doing, and went into a tent alone together. Awkward moment, anyone? We are invited to read into this silence. What was really said behind closed doors? The two men quietly disappearing into the tent points to the fact this was a time of reckoning. I have a feeling that just then Moses wished he could return to Egypt.[34]

The idea of Jewish men talking to each other about such moments of family tension, both within the same generation and beyond, may not seem likely. Much of the time that men interact they seem adversarial, whether across a table in a meeting or even joking competitively in a locker room. Rabbi Steven Leder, spiritual leader of Wilshire Boulevard Temple in Los Angeles, has written that men are "competitors, clients, or strangers." In today's world, men only seem to come together in exclusively all-male groups for competitive sports. Men do not necessarily think of each other as people. He confesses:

> For me and for so many others, to be a man among men meant to talk around things and keep my guard up; to carry the unique weight of manhood in mighty silence. Men are God's loneliest creatures.[35]

Despite the stereotypes of Jewish history and the pressures of modern society, the fact remains that Jewish men have a rich tradition that can serve as a guide through family life. We need rituals to mark events in our life: our education, our marriage, and our raising of children. People come to the synagogue to meet those needs, most often when children need to be enrolled in religious school but also at other thresholds, such as a geographical move or when one approaches retirement. Most rituals are about making connections. They are reasons to bring family and friends together to note that something in life has changed, that some significant event has occurred.

We need not validate Henry David Thoreau's observation that "the mass of men lead lives of quiet desperation."[36] Judaism teaches us that men should work in the context of community, fulfilling their responsibilities to their families and one another. Instead of Thoreau, who famously retreated into the Neverland of the woods of Walden, look to the Jewish Sage Hillel, who admonished, "Do not withdraw from the community" (*Pirkei Avot* 2:5). Being a spiritual Jewish man has never meant being a monk; Jewish life is not lived in isolation. We should especially remember this today when we can hide in an office, staring at a computer monitor for hours on end and imagining that we are connected to others. *Being truly connected means being present in the lives of others.*

As one Jewish man who benefits enormously from synagogue life, I know that there are better reasons to be Jewish than to stand together against antisemites. There are internal reasons that are a cause of celebration for being Jewish. Judaism has been the vocabulary and framework through which generations have loved, married, and raised children. It is a moral compass pointing to a transcendent reality. Jews who embrace their Judaism live rich and meaningful lives and are not at a loss when they cross life's varied thresholds. Most of all, you are never alone in a world that can often be lonely when you embrace the joy of being a part of a community. You know where and with whom you belong.

With connections come responsibilities. Men should be able to speak to each other from the heart. To look into other people's faces means to take responsibility for them. It means to see them as human beings, not as a means to an end. And it means others take responsibility for us as well, that we share life's burdens and challenges. This sharing of responsibility in the midst of community has a name in Hebrew: *b'rit*, or covenant. It is partnering with others to go beyond what we can do alone. It means being part of a team. Our Sages teach that through the faces of others there is holiness, from the arrival of a friend in a time of need to the glance of a loved one on an average day. Such were the words when Jacob was reunited with Esau after many years, each one a complete man, both aggressive and passive, beyond any stereotype: "To see your face is like seeing the face of God" (Genesis 33:10).

"BOYS PRETENDING TO BE MEN"

It remains true that men still have things to learn from other men and that boys can only learn some lessons from men and not their mothers. Girls, too, need to have male role models.

This does not contradict feminism. I consider myself a feminist in that I believe in the equal empowerment and opportunity of women in all spheres of life, especially in the religious world of which I am a part. I believe that God is above gender and that prayer books should be gender-inclusive. It does not change the fact, however, that men have a role to play as men for each other and in teaching the next generation.

The consequences of men being too busy to get involved in spiritual pursuits are many, not the least of which is personal loss. Men's spiritual needs are numerous and deep. Judaism contains a great deal of wisdom about what it means to be a mature man in today's world. Jewish teachings can guide us through our obligations to our parents, to our spouses, and to our children. Most importantly, Judaism can teach us about ourselves and how to make sure we conduct ourselves as men and not as boys. There are sacred teachings written by men for men, and these lessons are waiting to be learned. Feeling frantic at work and desperate at home is not the Jewish ideal of what a man's life should be. Jethro pulls Moses aside to speak to him privately in a tent; what if there had been no Jethro in Moses's life? What would have happened to Moses's relationship to his wife? His children? His growth as a leader?

The second consequence impacts the next generation. Both boys and girls need to learn from men as well as women. In our tradition, there have always been archetypal Jewish wise men who participated in showing the next generation the way into Jewish life. If a generation of men chooses to absent itself from the synagogue and other Jewish institutions, the example set will be that the things that give life meaning are to be found elsewhere. Surely, there is a deeper experience to be had in life than sitting together in front of the television watching sports, too tired to bother with a real conversation.

The third and most devastating consequence of Jewish men being cut off from their spirituality is that the world suffers for lack of mature men. Consider this reflection by psychologists Robert Moore and Douglas Gillette:

> The drug dealer, the ducking and diving political leader, the wife beater, the chronically "crabby" boss, the "hot shot" junior executive, the unfaithful husband, the company "yes man," the indifferent graduate school adviser, the "holier than thou" minister, the gang member, the father who can never find the time to attend his daughter's school programs, the coach who ridicules his star athletes … all these men have something in common. They are all boys pretending to be men.[37]

Our world is in desperate need of mature men to address unprecedented problems. Thoughtful, spiritual men need to understand and act on their responsibilities. The Jewish people has proudly produced such men for centuries. Past generations of Jews have disproportionately contributed to the goodness of the world. They were able to do so, I believe, because they were grounded in the values of Jewish tradition.[38] Jewish people make up less than 1 percent of the world's population but over 20 percent of the world's Nobel Prize winners.[39] The values and education that these individuals received in their homes and synagogues make their Jewishness no mere coincidence. The Sages of antiquity were optimistic that that we can grow as human beings, meet the needs of our families, and contribute to the greater good.

Freed from the stereotypes of Jewish men, we can fulfill the mitzvah, *the sacred obligation, to seek Jewish wisdom, informed by both tradition and each person's own unique relationship to God.*

Questions for Reflection

- How is your life at work the same or different from your father's or grandfather's? Your time at home? Your relationship, if any, to a synagogue?

- Why do you think the Nazis portrayed Jewish men as effeminate? Why did early Zionists portray Jewish men living in the Diaspora as weak?

- List historical and contemporary Jewish men you consider physically powerful, even "macho."

- How does ambivalence over being Jewish impact the Jewish men you know? Yourself?

- How do you balance being a responsible man to your loved ones while fulfilling the obligations of your work? When are the times of greatest pressure?

- When is the last time you considered your spiritual needs?

Fill in this card and return it to us to be eligible for our quarterly drawing for a $100 gift certificate for Jewish Lights books.

We hope that you will enjoy this book and find it useful in enriching your life.

Book title:

Your comments:

How you learned of this book:

If purchased: Bookseller _____ City _____ State _____

Please send me a free JEWISH LIGHTS Publishing catalog. I am interested in: (check all that apply)

1. ❏ Spirituality
2. ❏ Mysticism/Kab>alah
3. ❏ Philosophy/Theology
4. ❏ History/Politics

5. ❏ Women's Interest
6. ❏ Environmental Interest
7. ❏ Healing/Recovery
8. ❏ Children's Books

9. ❏ Caregiving/Grieving
10. ❏ Ideas for Book Groups
11. ❏ Religious Education Resources
12. ❏ Interfaith Resources

Name (PRINT) _____

Street _____

City _____ State _____ Zip _____

E-MAIL (FOR SPECIAL OFFERS ONLY) _____

Please send a JEWISH LIGHTS Publishing catalog to my friend:

Name (PRINT) _____

Street _____

City _____ State _____ Zip _____

JEWISH LIGHTS PUBLISHING

Tel: (802) 457-4000 • Fax: (802) 457-4004

Available at better booksellers. Visit us online at www.jewishlights.com

WIN A $100 GIFT CERTIFICATE!

Fill in this card and
mail it to us—
or fill it in online at
**jewishlights.com/
feedback.html**

—to be eligible for a
$100 gift certificate for
Jewish Lights books.

3
Growing Up and Being a Son

I can remember as a teenager taking the family car to a party without my parents' permission. There was exhilaration in the rebellion, and also great fear. My thoughts came rapidly: I had defied my parents' will. I was free. I was independent. Oh God—what happens if I have an accident or get a speeding ticket?

In retrospect, it must have been a comical scene: a nervous teenager behind the wheel of a red Ford creeping along at twenty miles an hour toward a friend's house. Even in defiance, the commandments instilled in me since birth kicked in: "Honor your father and your mother" (Exodus 20:12), or perhaps more to the point, "Fear your mother and your father" (Leviticus 19:3). Any pleasure I got out of having the car was drained by the guilt of knowing I was lying and the terror of being caught.

I managed to lose my fear at the party. Everything was going great. But as I backed out to leave, I managed to dent the side of the car, right near the gas cap, by striking a short tree planted near the driveway. The branches scraped the paint into little filings. The dent, however, was immediately apparent. I looked at it from different angles, trying to pretend that it really wasn't there. A friend suggested that if I used a plunger, I could somehow pop the dent back out. I went back to the party and asked for a plunger.

"A plunger?" My friend asked.

"Yeah, from your bathroom toilet," I said. When he continued to look confused, I clarified, "You know, for my car."

There I was, with most of the people coming outside from the party to watch, as I frantically worked the plunger in a desperate attempt to remove the incriminating evidence. Needless to say, it didn't work.

It is decades later, and someone related a different kind of story about stealing his father's car, only in this case he did so as an adult. The difference between the two thefts was that I was acting like a boy, while my friend acted like a man:

> It was near Dad's eighty-fifth birthday that we stole his car. He really shouldn't have been driving, but we didn't know how to take the car from him. We knew he wouldn't give up the keys without a fight. God forbid that he should have hit somebody while he was out on the road. He had no business driving, and we all knew it. His reflexes were not what they once were. But taking the car away was a big step. It robbed him of his independence, his self-esteem. He was not going to go along with this quietly. So we arranged for the car to be stolen. We called the sheriff to let him know what we were doing. And one day, when we knew Dad was busy and not looking, the car disappeared. Of course, Dad called the police. He ranted for a while. The sheriff went along with it. Later, I told Dad that I needed the car's title for some paperwork. And that was that. Dad died without knowing that the car was hidden in my cousin's garage.[1]

As a boy, I broke the commandment to respect my parents, but my friend fulfilled the duty of honoring his father. He found a way to take the car from him, possibly saving his life as well as others, while preserving his father's dignity.

Many of us are not so creative. It is difficult to find a way to be the kind of son we aspire to be. Part of growing up is to shift from taking from our parents to giving to them. As these two stories illustrate, the boy acts for himself, but the man acts on behalf of another.

BIBLICAL BOYS AND MEN

Before I talk about being a son, let me discuss being a boy.

The quintessential Bible story about boys is that of Joseph and his brothers, which is the longest in the book of Genesis and very popular as a children's tale. Made even more popular by Andrew Lloyd Webber, generations of adults and Sunday school children have been entertained by performances of *Joseph and the Amazing Technicolor Dreamcoat*, which recounts Joseph's rise from rags to riches. Behind this suspenseful adaptation, however, is the story found in the Hebrew Bible. The original tale extends beyond just the figure of Joseph to include Joseph's brother Judah, from whom the term "Judaism" is derived.

The biblical version of the story begins with a man named Jacob, also called Israel, who is the head of a large family. Jacob's family, including two wives, two handmaids (essentially second-class wives), twelve boys, and one girl are traditionally regarded as the ancestors of the Jewish people. Jacob singles out with his affection Joseph, the son of his most beloved wife, Rachel. As a sign of his favoritism, he gives Joseph "an ornamented tunic," which acts, in effect, as a target for his brothers' envy. The Torah says that they could not speak a peaceable word to him (Genesis 37:3–4).

Imagine this family. Picture the doting father, the preoccupied mother, and the incredibly talented and arrogant favorite son. Intoxicated with his father's love and strutting around in his colorful coat, Joseph dreams of greatness for himself. He dreams of his brothers bowing down and serving him. Under the protection of his father's favoritism, he boasts of his dreams, and his brothers hate him all the more. "Hear this dream which I have dreamed," he says (Genesis 37:6). Even in the face of their hatred, he continues to brag about his visions of greatness for himself at their expense. He feels as if he is God's chosen one.

What might have been normal sibling rivalry takes a tragic twist when the brothers conspire to murder Joseph. But rather than do the deed themselves, they throw him into a pit without food or water. Eventually Judah comes up with the idea to sell Joseph as a slave to a passing caravan of Ishmaelites headed to Egypt. The brothers take the money and assume Joseph will die in servitude. To cover their crime, they take Joseph's coat, smear it with blood, and bring it to their father. "God's chosen" is gone.

Fast-forward many years.

In Egypt, Joseph experiences the hardships of slavery and prison. His arrogance evaporates in the face of real-life suffering. Nevertheless, he uses the talents that God gave him to raise himself up. When faced with possible transgressions, the Talmud, a collection of teachings by the Rabbis from 200 to 500 CE, says Joseph "envisions the face of his father" and stays on a righteous path (Babylonian Talmud, *Sotah* 36b).[2] Eventually, the land of Egypt is threatened with famine, and it is Joseph who is called from prison and devises a strategy to store food. Joseph saves thousands of lives. His service to Pharaoh makes him the second most important official in Egypt. In many ways, his dreams come true. But Joseph has learned his place: he sees himself as one of many servants to God in a larger plan, not the central actor. "Not I, [but] God" becomes his constant refrain (Genesis 41:16).

Meanwhile, Joseph's brother Judah has returned home to live with the crime of having disposed of his brother. He also faces the task of keeping his family together. He grows up, also learning some hard lessons. He discovers that getting rid of one favorite son only produces another. Their father now dotes on the youngest child, Benjamin.

The brothers are reunited when Judah and the rest of the brothers are struck by the famine and have to go to Egypt to beg for food. They unwittingly present themselves before a man they do not recognize as Joseph. They speak to him and tell him of their family, especially how their father is old and frail. They also admit that their brother Benjamin is their father's new favorite. In hearing that history has repeated itself, Joseph devises a scheme to see if they have changed since their childhood days. He holds Benjamin hostage, offering the brothers money in exchange for Benjamin becoming Joseph's slave. Will they repeat the sins of their past? Will they sell another son favored by their father into slavery?

Judah steps forward. He looks this Egyptian madman in the eye and tells him he may not do this. If he takes Benjamin as a slave, their father will die of grief. No amount of money can right the wrong. In a bold confrontation, Judah stands up for his brother. In fact, he offers his own life in exchange: "Please let your servant remain as a slave to my lord instead of the boy, and let the boy go back with his brothers" (Genesis 44:33).

In response to this display of love and responsibility, Joseph breaks down and confesses, "I am your brother Joseph, he whom you sold into Egypt. Now, do not be distressed or reproach yourselves because you sold me hither; it was to save life that God sent me ahead of you" (Genesis 45:4–5).

WHAT "RESPONSIBLE" MEANS

As children, we all have fantasies. Once we grasped the world with chubby fists, believing we were the center of the universe. Joseph's coat is a symbol of narcissism, of the extreme self-absorption of childhood when we believe we are a law unto ourselves. The narcissism of childhood is supposed to eventually develop into a humbler version of self-love, a love that enables us to love others. Judith Viorst explains the ideal:

> For healthy growth involves being able to … give up our grandiosity and make do with a human-proportioned self. It means that although we may, in the course of our life, be beset by emotional difficulties, we possess a reliable self, a sense of identity.[3]

Siblings bring the challenge of sharing love, something that children often cannot immediately comprehend. Judah and the rest of the brothers indulge their fantasy of disposing of the competition, known to us when an older child asks when we are going to bring the new baby back to the hospital. As children, we cannot understand that one day our siblings will not be our rivals but our allies, that memories of pain will fade, and deeper connections of love and respect can grow. We all begin, however, thinking our parents are gods, the Perfect Ones who are bigger, stronger, wiser, and can fix anything, even as they satisfy our every whim and provide us every pleasure.

All these fantasies are present in the Joseph and Judah story. As a child, Joseph dreams of the entire universe—not just his brothers but also his parents, who are like "the sun [and] the moon" (Genesis 37:9)—bowing before him. Judah dreams of getting rid of Joseph, most likely so he can become his father's favorite. And both believe that their father, a patriarch carrying forward his ancestors' covenant, does not just speak for God but is God Himself. The fallible love of their father could not live up to their idealized vision of him and must have struck the boys as profoundly unfair.

Wrapped up in ourselves, as we all are when we enter this world, we strive for independence and power. But we gain much more by eventually letting go of our narcissistic longings and impossible expectations. Joseph gains a spiritual sense of mission, that God has a place for him in this world, perhaps not at the center of the universe but in an important and powerful position nonetheless. Judah gains the leadership of his family. Through offering his life, he becomes his brother's keeper (Genesis 4:9). Both Judah and Joseph discover they are able to see their father in a new light, not as God but as God's servant. The fallible old man is still a man of wisdom, a person of guidance who did his imperfect best to raise them and teach them to walk their own path. Love is often unfair, but that does not excuse us from our responsibilities.

Responsible means that we make and keep commitments. Responsible means, of course, that we tie our own shoes. But it also means that we are not allowed to blame our terrible childhood—or passion, temptation, ignorance, or innocence—for acts that are ours, for deeds that we did indeed do. For if, in fact, we do them, we are responsible.[4]

The reconciliation of Joseph and Judah represents a loss and a gain. Lost is the illusion that we are important, all-powerful, and in full control of our destiny. This is a painful discovery, and boys may cling to the illusion to avoid the pain, remaining boys even as they physically become men. But the reconciliation of Judah and Joseph also represents the gain of responsibility, love, meaning, insight, and support. It means no longer blaming our childhood for our misfortunes, and accepting our imperfections and the flaws encountered in others. It is the gain of men coming together and accepting who we are.

A midrash, or Rabbinic exposition, embellishes the story of Joseph and Judah. Eventually, their father Jacob dies, and together all the sons bury him. As they return from the funeral, the brothers see Joseph walk off the road to a pit, the very pit into which they threw him as a child before selling him into slavery. The brothers tremble, fearing Joseph's childhood fury will be rekindled. Joseph, however, reassures them: "I wanted to say a blessing for the miracle that happened to me, starting right here in this place" (*Tanchuma Vayechi* 17).

Boy Psychology, Man Psychology, and the *Yetzer*

The Sages of Judaism created a clear divide between carefree boyhood and the point at which a male is responsible for keeping God's commandments and becoming his "brother's keeper" (Genesis 4:9), which is age thirteen. It is at this point that he can be counted in a *minyan*, lead the congregation in prayer, be called to the Torah, fast on Yom Kippur, and participate fully in all of Judaism's sacred rituals. These responsibilities do not mean the boy is suddenly a man; rather, they delineate the end of childhood. American culture, in comparison, has various legal thresholds to delineate the various stages of maturity: sixteen to drive, eighteen to vote and serve in the armed forces, and twenty-one to drink alcohol.

As clear a distinction as a birthday may be, we know that the road to manhood is more a fluid process than a sharp departure. It is for this reason that some psychologists distinguish between "boy psychology" and "man psychology," that is, thinking like a boy and thinking like a mature man. Grown immature men abound, and the true test of manhood is not a birthday party but a change in how we think about ourselves and the world around us.

Psychologists Douglas Gillette and Robert Moore use archetypes, models, or images of commonly held ideas to describe how a boy might think. A boy is a "high-chair tyrant" who demands that others feed, kiss, and serve him. When he is not throwing a tantrum, he is either silent or whiny.[5] He enjoys manipulating others and asks questions to show everyone how smart he is instead of to gain information. He feels good when he is able to point out where another went wrong. He is alternatively a bully or a coward, depending on his fear of the power of those around him. He is unaware of his own limitations and struggles to dominate others and his own behavior and emotions. All of these qualities can lead to daring behavior that is self-destructive and immature.[6]

Man psychology, Gillette and Moore continue, is concerned with things beyond the self. Men are able to be generous and give to others. They are able to "act decisively and with courage." They can be deeply reflective and clear-sighted, and they exhibit a "convinced connectedness to all things."[7]

The Sages of Judaism state these insights another way. They believe we all come into this world with our animalistic instincts to fight, flee, and feel erotic pleasure fully formed. None of these instincts are bad in and of themselves, but they can lead to destructive behaviors. As children, our animal drives, the *yetzer ra,* direct our actions, and we are not morally responsible. It is only with maturity and training, with thoughtful spiritual reflection, that our impulse for good, the *yetzer tov,* is revealed and nurtured when we reach age thirteen (*Avot d'Rabbi Natan* 16).[8] The good impulse, they teach, takes time and training to cultivate. We as adults have both impulses, with the boyhood *yetzer ra* advocating selfishness and arrogance and the mature *yetzer tov* advocating *menschlichkeit,* Yiddish for "manliness," and signifying decency, humility, and generosity.

Who Is a Man?

The Sage Ben Zoma taught the difference between boyhood and manhood in a series of ironic questions (*Pirkei Avot* 4:1). He asked, "Who is wise? Who is strong? Who is rich? And who is honored?" The boy would say the wise person is the one who knows the most. He is able to out-debate others, show where they are faulty, and get the highest grades in school. He has the top position in the university, has the highest degrees, and relishes showing how smart he is at every opportunity. The man, however, answers the question "Who is wise?" with the response, "The one who learns from everyone." Regarding all people as his teachers, a man asks questions to learn, and shows respect for all.

"Who is strong?" The boy believes that strength comes through might. The strongest person is the one who commands the most powerful army or has the biggest muscles. He can dominate and control others, and people fear his wrath. However, the man answers, "Who is strong? The one who controls his impulses." Strength is defined as self-control, not power over others. Inner discipline allows a man to be true to himself and dependable. By establishing himself with integrity, the man learns a sense of balance, so he can face life with confidence and serve as an anchor for those who rely upon him.

"Who is rich?" The boy clearly values having as much money and possessions as possible. A bumper sticker reads, "He who dies with the most toys wins." With riches also comes fame. Money buys him recognition, access to pleasure, and prominence. But the man answers, "Who is rich? The one content with his lot." Through a deep sense of satisfaction, the man is able to appreciate the gift of each new day and the miracles of life that surround us at all times, no matter how modest the circumstances.

Finally, "Who is honored?" The boy seeks gratification of his ego by getting others to love him. He wants to be liked by everyone, and he feels insecure if they do not compliment him or pay him attention. But the man says, "Who is honored? The one who honors others." The man treats others as being made in God's image and having inherent worth. His honor comes from his character, and he does not stoop to the level of others who behave badly. His values are drawn from a sense of responsibility, the standard by which he measures himself.

It is only with reflection and guidance that we learn to learn from others, that we are able to exhibit self-control, that we feel contentment and can honor another without any thought of ourselves. It takes time, effort, and education to become a civilized human being. For Jews, that education is in the wisdom of Torah.

To ignore the wisdom of our ancestors is to invite a prolonged if not permanent adolescence. The last thing the world needs is more childish behavior from people who are supposed to be adults.

A father or other male role model is not always available to show a boy how to cultivate his *yetzer tov*. Without positive male role models, boys learn to be men from their surrounding culture. Today that often means receiving conflicting messages from the media that portrays "ideal men" in destructive ways:

The image of the male as strong is confused with the image of the male as aggressive and violent. Virility has been replaced with promiscuity. Adventurousness has evolved into recklessness. Intelligence is often confused with bravado and arrogance.[9]

In 1998, researchers at McLean Hospital in Boston found that adolescent males showed a great deal of confusion over what was expected of them. They accepted gender egalitarianism but also felt that "guys must be sure of themselves" and "men are always ready for sex." They felt pressure to mask feelings of low self-esteem and were worried about loneliness and isolation. Over half of those surveyed felt "daily shame" due to taunts about their masculinity and were prone to depression.[10] Without mature, positive male role models, these feelings can create serious obstacles to manhood.

HEROES AND OLD WISE MEN

Returning to the biblical story of Joseph and Judah, we discover that this parable follows a pattern found in many other stories from around the world. The story focuses on the hero, an archetype deeply imbedded in humanity's unconscious. The hero is a figure who keeps popping up in stories despite radical differences in time, language, and culture and has much to do with how we understand manhood.

According to a well-established pattern in literature, the hero figure comes from royal parentage, often with some kind of unusual conception, such as overcoming infertility or a parent's prayer to conceive a child. The hero's life is endangered in some way in his youth—he may be abandoned, for example—forcing him to leave and grow up far from home. As he grows, he encounters obstacles, but he finds a wise old man who helps him overcome the challenges and teaches him some form of wisdom. The hero then returns home and claims his rightful place as king.[11]

The biblical figure of Joseph fits this general pattern. Joseph is born through prayerful intervention when his mother, Rachel, is infertile. His life is threatened by his brothers, and so he is raised in Egypt. Joseph faces trials while in Egypt, but the lessons of the

covenant of his father, symbolized in revelations and dream interpretation, raise him up in stature. He then establishes his authority
as viceroy of Egypt. Joseph returns home, first to bury his father
and then by making his brothers swear not to bury him in a foreign
land but to return his body to the land of his ancestors.

In addition to the Joseph narrative, the stories of Moses, Oedipus, Perseus, Jesus, King Arthur, and Harry Potter, to name just a
few, also reenact this pattern to varying degrees. What always seems
to hover in the background of the hero story is the figure of the
wise old man. Joseph learns piety from the covenant of his father.
Moses learns responsibility from his father-in-law Jethro. Oedipus
learns from the Oracle at Delphi. Perseus is aided by the gods Her-
mes, Athena, and his father, Zeus. Jesus communes with his father
in heaven. King Arthur is tutored by the magician Merlin. Harry
Potter visits Dumbledore's office. Other heroes also have their wise
old men: David has Nathan, Sigurd has Odin, and Ivanhoe has King
Richard. Heroes cannot fully be heroes without their wise old men.
Analytical psychologist Carl Jung believed this was an integral part
of humanity's understanding of a boy's need for male guidance:

> Graybeard and boy belong together.... The wise old man
> appears in dreams in the guise of a magician, doctor, priest,
> teacher, professor, grandfather, or any other person pos-
> sessing authority.... The old man always appears when the
> hero is in a hopeless and desperate situation from which
> only profound reflection or a lucky idea ... can extricate
> him. But since, for internal and external reasons, the hero
> cannot accomplish this himself, the knowledge needed to
> compensate the deficiency comes in the form of a personi-
> fied thought, i.e., in the shape of this sagacious and helpful
> old man.[12]

Perhaps these stories are so powerful because men recognize this
not only as a pattern in literature but also in life. Boys grow up,
longing for their own form of heroism, their secret identity that

they fervently want the world to recognize. They rebel and leave home ready to claim a standing of their own. The term "Oedipus complex" refers in part to the feelings that one must overthrow one's father in order to win the kingdom. But boys, no matter the depth of their rebelliousness, desperately need the wisdom of older men to guide them. Heroes without wise mentors become stuck. Eventually, they strive to return home as men, on their own two feet, with their own accomplishments and confidence in themselves to establish their own house or kingdom.

A father is the natural figure to fill the role of the wise old man. The image of dad seated in his chair—a stand-in for a throne—at the head of the Seder table, leading the family through the Passover rite, can bring tears to the eyes. Ideally, when help is needed, the father is there to generously provide it. When big questions need answers, the father's advice is sought. A son's rebellion is expected and does not sever the relationship. The hero can wander far and wide, confident that there is a place called home to which he can always return for rest, safety, and reflection.

Of course, we cannot underestimate the equal and critical influence of a boy's mother. Her love, encouragement, nurturing, and support are as necessary as the milk she provides from her breast. But somewhere between the ages of three and five, developmental psychologists say boys begin to separate from mother and go in search of father to begin building "a sense of self."[13] For a boy trying to learn how to be a man, learning to be a son to his father is the first step. It is as if father and son are playing in the backyard, and the boy is given the football with the goal line behind Daddy. "You have to get through me first," Daddy says. That is true in more ways than one.

As a rabbi, I have been blessed to hear eulogies for fathers given by grateful sons who feel blessed with having had not only a provider but also a guide. "My father was my best friend," one man said to me. "He taught me everything of importance that I know." How someone is remembered is often a moment of truth for the quality of a life. I have heard many sons speak of their fathers with thankfulness and awe. "He was a tough soldier but a gentle soul," another son told a gathering. "He taught me how to ride a bike, running alongside, and then later taught me how to drive. He also taught me the values of honesty, hard work, and that family always comes first. He was proud of his Jewish heritage and always had a desire for learning. He was a wonderful father."

But it is not always this way.

THE ABUSIVE FATHER

I once visited a town in Michigan with a very small Jewish community and no rabbi. I went there because a Jewish man had died, and a cousin wanted a rabbi to officiate at the funeral. I found the address where his children had gathered and knocked on the door at the appointed time. We were to meet and talk about Dad so that I could write a eulogy. I knew something was wrong when they took a very long time to come to the door and after letting me in took another half hour before they were willing to sit in the same room with me.

"I am really only here to make sure that the bastard is really dead," one of the sons said to me. Others spoke of their father's narcissism, his selfishness, and of drunken fights in the house. My eulogy could not speak of the man as he was. Sometimes we grieve for the man who was our father, and sometimes we grieve for the father we wish we had.

At Jewish funerals, the family often participates in the burial by shoveling the first scoops of earth on top of the casket. The children of this man did so not out of reverence but out of a desire to bury the past and seek closure for themselves. They shoveled frantically.

Relationships between fathers and sons especially are emotionally loaded. Often, boys must seek other mentors, such as a stepfather, uncle, coach, college professor, clergy member, or teacher. Frequently, boys find a combination thereof. But the first stop always is the father, for better or worse.

What if Joseph and Judah did not learn of God from their father, Jacob, over whose love they fought? What if the son cannot talk to his father or the father cannot talk to him? What if the old man is abusive or absent? What if he is not, as Jung put it, "sagacious and helpful"?

Abuse by parents can be more than just physical hurt. Abuse can be emotional, when a parent continually belittles a child, destroys their self-esteem, and kills their spirit. It can take sinister forms of withholding finances or sabotaging dreams. Abuse can be as obvious as publicly humiliating a child or forcing them to be something they are not. All of these are forms of violence. More will be said about domestic abuse in the discussion about being a partner in marriage.

The biblical tale of Samuel and Saul cautions us. Saul is chosen by God to meet the people's desire for a king, and he becomes the first monarch of Israel. But Samuel the prophet does not like this. He feels the people should be content with God as their king and him as their prophet. Samuel, as a counselor to the new monarch, is supposed to be the boy's teacher and guide. He is supposed to advise and aid. But Samuel's intentions are clear even before Saul becomes ruler. Before he anoints Saul, Samuel sets him up for failure. Samuel tells the people exactly what he thinks their new king will do. He tells them the new king will steal their sons and make them into servants to run alongside his chariots and to fight in his army. He will abduct their daughters and make them serve in his kitchens. He will also create taxes, seizing their best harvests and most valuable possessions. In the end, the king is going to drain them of all they hold dear.

This is the introduction that Samuel makes for the new king, Saul (1 Samuel 8:11–18). We can imagine that if he was introducing him as a speaker, there would have been more shock than applause. Samuel seems to feel so threatened and bitter about his replacement that instead of being a teacher and guide, he lays an inescapable trap for Saul. Samuel's actions are cruel.

Saul never stands a chance. Sabotaged by Samuel, Saul never commands the people's respect. As king, he goes from failure to failure, trying to please Samuel and the God he serves. In the end, the kingdom is taken from him. Saul is a damaged, tragic figure, suffering from depression and violent outbursts. His rule ends in suicide.

Some of us are fortunate to have father figures who are nurturing guides, who let us rebel but do not let go, who try to pass on life's lessons as best they can. Some of us are not.

Naming Our Fathers

No man is perfect. Fathers and sons are notorious for their rough-and-tumble relationships. Is it because fathers naturally see their sons as rivals? Is it because sons seem to feel the need to "outdo" their fathers, to overthrow them in some way?

As boys grow older, they need to come to terms with who their father was during their childhood and who he was not. Psychologist Samuel Osherson claims that each of us must "name our father," which is a "coming to terms with who he really is, stripped of the distortions of childhood."[14] The images of men and masculinity internalized as we grow are "a composite of fantasy and reality,"[15] often constructed to rationalize why one's father was absent. Men experience what has been called "father hunger,"[16] regardless of whether the father was constantly away at work or simply emotionally distant. This problem is exacerbated by the frequency of divorce. With some fathers only available on weekends or some other custody arrangement, more distance is created and therefore more challenges. Fathers may struggle with guilt and shame; both father and child may experience emptiness and longing. Our spirits wrestle with filling in the gaps in the father-child relationship, creating a picture in our minds of what we think our father is feeling, with little opportunity to ever truly know.

Perhaps we experienced father as all-suffering, the man who hardly ever came home from work, who never had time to relax, who carried his family as a burden. Perhaps we experienced him as needing our help, where we conspired with our mothers to deceive and protect him and his self-esteem. Perhaps we saw him as angry, viewing his children as his competitors. With all of these possible projections, it is likely that very few sons grow up knowing the inner life of the man who was dad.[17]

"The Two of Them Walked On Together"

A father spoke on the *bimah* (stage) at his son's bar mitzvah, and as he addressed his son (giving the usual compliments about not only the "great job that you did today," but also his son's prowess on the soccer field), he remarked as an aside that their best conversations always seem to take place in the car. It occurred to me that many men, and most likely fathers and sons, speak most personally in the car. The question is why, and the answer appears to be that while in the car they do not have to face each other. Looking out the windshield in the same direction, the two never have to make eye contact and therefore risk more intimacy than they feel they can handle. A small personal offering is given; the true inner life remains hidden away.

Consider another passage from the Torah of a father and son, also traveling side by side. The trip is a momentous and unimaginable one. In Genesis, Abraham travels to sacrifice his son Isaac at the call of God. The Torah says that the "two walked on together." The only dialogue between the two is brief. Isaac calls to Abraham, "Father!" and Abraham answers, "Here I am, my son." Isaac looks around and sees the wood and the flint knife, but he does not see the animal for the sacrifice. In bewilderment, he asks, "Where is the sheep?" Abraham answers that God will provide the ram. The Torah then says again that "the two of them walked on together" (Genesis 22:6–8).

The repeated phrase "the two of them walked on together" highlights the irony of this passage. They walk side by side, facing the same direction, but the son cannot look into his father's eyes or heart. Here, the two figures, the father and the son, are supposed to be "together," yet the son has no idea what is really on the father's mind. Isaac asks, but Abraham sidesteps. Is Abraham blinded by the pain of what he feels he must do? Does he feel rage? Sadness? Does he believe that God will not let him do it? Like Isaac, we can never know. Abraham's silence is the most characteristic feature of the story.

Isaac remains silent after this exchange as well. Is he in awe of his father? Trusting? Fearful? Can he possibly understand the God that his father worships or the faith that moves him? Rabbi W. Gunther Plaut claims that "the story may thus be read as a paradigm of a father-and-son relationship. In a way all parents seek to dominate their child and are in danger of seeking to sacrifice them to parental plans or hopes."[18]

At the moment of truth, God tells Abraham not to hurt or even touch the boy; Abraham is not allowed to lay a finger on Isaac. Abraham immediately stops and sacrifices the ram provided by God in Isaac's stead. The story culminates in this lesson of spiritually giving our children to God and God's commandments but not through physical sacrifice. Yet we read later, at the conclusion of the story, that Abraham, and Abraham alone, returns from the mountain. "Abraham then returned to his servants" (Genesis 22:19). Where has Isaac gone? We do not know. It is left unsaid. We only know that the two of them are no longer together.

Must boys seek to separate completely from their father and from his hopes and dreams? But can they recognize the man beyond his imperfections, affirming the covenant that he tries to pass on? The Torah points us in the direction of reconciliation. While not much more is said of this story in the Bible, what is said is significant. Even after this traumatic event, Isaac not only survives but flourishes. Abraham continues to reach out to his son, going so far as to arrange a match for him for marriage. Isaac also appears to bury his father with honor. He becomes prosperous and raises his own family. The Torah tells us that Isaac "dug anew the wells which had been dug in the days of his father Abraham" (Genesis 26:18). God also appears to Isaac and tells him, "I am the God of your father Abraham. Fear not, for I am with you" (Genesis 26:24). In response, Isaac builds an altar and worships, renewing the covenant. In some fashion, we see that Isaac has found peace with his father as well as his role in being a man.

Our fathers are imperfect people. Many men carry around wounded images of their father (and what it means to be a man) inside of them. Yet even the most abusive or neglectful father must be named and honored as such, as a father, so that the son can grow and become his own man and decide which parts of his father's life he wishes to emulate and which parts he wishes to leave behind. The son must decide what kind of human being he wishes to be.

It is instructive that one of the Ten Commandments is to "honor your father and your mother" (Exodus 20:12). It does not say to imitate, praise, or even love. Perhaps for some that would be going too far. But the Sages had a clear idea of what, at a minimum, "honoring" meant and deemed it a healthy responsibility incumbent upon us all. As one Jewish philosopher understands it, the commandments exist to make us into better people.[19]

Honoring and Fearing

As I noted earlier, there are two different commandments in the Torah regarding one's parents. The first, and more well known, is "Honor your father and your mother" (Exodus 20:12). The second is "You shall each fear his mother and his father" (Leviticus 19:3).

One commandment tells us to "honor," and the other commands us to "fear." The question is, what do "honor" and "fear" mean? How do we show respect for our parents? Are we really supposed to be afraid of them? The Talmud explains honor as "taking care of" and fear as "holding in awe":

Our Rabbis taught: What is "fear" and what is "honor"? Fear means that he [his son] must neither stand nor sit in his [the father's] place, nor contradict his words, nor tip the scales against him [in a public argument]. Honor means

> that he must give him food and drink, clothe and cover him,
> lead him in and out. (Babylonian Talmud, *Kiddushin* 31b)

The Rabbis of antiquity had a very practical understanding of honor and fear. One showed these dispositions through actions. The father and the son, as the chief wielders of wealth and power in an ancient patriarchal society, were the primary audience for Rabbinic teaching. Fear meant a show of respect; not occupying a father's rightful place or publicly contradicting and embarrassing him were ways of showing reverence for a father's wisdom and dignity. I imagine such fear to be different from what we feel at physical danger (although certainly discipline not too long ago happened with a rod or belt). Instead, fear here seems to mean fear of violating the boundaries of one's proper place.

In a contemporary understanding, we might still feel fear at the thought of taking our father's place in a more literal sense, not by sitting where he usually sits but by taking on his role. Will we do any better than he did? What kind of father will I be or have I been? What is it truly like to walk in his shoes?

Added to this is the fear of disappointing our parents. If we hold our parents in high esteem, then we might be afraid of failing to reach the goals they set for us. One man remarked to me that his fear of his father was similar to the fear he felt at "disappointing coach." As a basketball player, one look at his coach shaking his head when he failed to give it his all was enough to fill him with shame. A simple look was devastating.

The Rabbis' definition of fear seems to apply to us in our youth, just as their definition of honor has more to do with the time when our parents are older. Honoring, according to the Rabbis, means taking care of their basic needs. We show honor by providing food and drink, clothing, and transportation. Honor, according to this definition, means that when our parents are no longer able to take care of themselves, we provide for them as they provided for us as children. Even if they did not do so adequately, by honoring them in this way we strive to be better people.

Another aspect of these two commandments is the order in which one's parents are mentioned in the Torah. In honoring, the father comes first, and in fearing, the emphasis is placed on the mother. The Talmud explains that this tries to make up for a deficiency in nature. We might naturally fear our fathers more than our mothers, perhaps because stereotypically father is a voice of authority and discipline. Honoring mother may seem easier, because again, according to the stereotype, she is the one we might more readily go to with a problem; she's the compassionate nurturer. For this reason, the Torah tries to rebalance the natural tendency, reminding us to honor our fathers as well as fear them, and to fear our mothers as well as honor them (Babylonian Talmud, *Kiddushin* 30b–31a). In all this, the Torah tells us that God has a large stake:

> There are three partners in each human being—the Holy Blessed One, the father, and the mother. When one honors one's father and mother, the Holy Blessed One says: "I consider it as though I lived with them and they honored Me." (Babylonian Talmud, *Kiddushin* 30b)

In this way, the Sages drew a line connecting the honor due parents and the honor due God. Certainly to children, their parents are "godlike" in their power and influence. Disobeying a father or mother (as we all do eventually) has enormous emotional consequences.

When Disobeying Your Parents Is a *Mitzvah*

Is the commandment to honor and fear, and therefore obey, one's father and mother absolute? The answer is no. Jewish law elaborates that one cannot obey one's parents if they order you to break one of God's commandments. Our parents may be godlike, but they are not God. For instance, Jewish law states that if a father orders you not to reconcile with someone with whom there is a family grievance, you are to ignore your father's command, for forgiveness is precious to God (*Shulchan Aruch, Yoreh Deah* 240:15).

But there is another limit to the commandment to honor, one people face every day as their parents live longer lives. Today, taking care of elderly parents is far from simple. Institutions abound to assist older people, from "active living" communities for seniors, to assisted living campuses, to nursing homes. Our options used to be few. You either cared for an elderly parent in your house or put them in a nursing home, where they often received questionable care. The guilt we may feel over relying on an institution to provide care for a parent can be tremendous. Our current situation gives this instruction from Jewish law a particularly contemporary ring:

> If one's father or mother becomes demented, one should endeavor to act with them in accordance to their mental condition until God has mercy upon them. However, if the son can no longer bear it because their situation is severe, he may leave them and delegate others to take care of them. (*Shulchan Aruch, Yoreh Deah* 240:10)

There are limits to what we can do for our parents. We can provide for them the best we know how. We can love them if they experience the second childhood that often comes with old age as their mind journeys to a less comprehending place. But God does not want us to sacrifice our lives for them. As one ancient source put it, we are to live by the commandments, not die by them (Babylonian Talmud, *Sanhedrin* 74a). The duty to be a good son does not mean meeting impossible expectations.

The Mishnah, the earliest compilation of Rabbinic law from around the year 200 CE, states:

> [If there is a choice between searching] for something you lost or for something your father lost, your own takes precedence. (*Mishnah Bava Metzia* 2:11)

We must strive to balance our needs and the needs of our parents. If the choice must be made between our survival and the survival of a parent, in that extreme situation the Mishnah would have us choose life for ourselves. If the "something lost" is our hopes and dreams versus theirs, you are entitled to pursue your own dreams first. You are not supposed to lose yourself on behalf of your parents. They may not command that kind of extreme devotion.

This cautionary boundary is not an invitation to selfishness; this only applies in matters of physical and emotional survival. You are supposed to behave toward your parents with generosity and love. Nevertheless, it is important to note that the need to honor your parents does not mean to accept abuse or martyrdom. You honor them best when you live your life fully in the ways that God commands. Your moral behavior is the real testimony to your ancestors, even beyond your parents.

BEING *ZEIDE* IN A CULTURE THAT WORSHIPS YOUTH

If you are fortunate enough to have a living grandparent, it is important to note that all of the duties to honor and fear your parents apply to them as well. In addition, there is the commandment to "rise before the aged and show deference to the old" (Leviticus 19:32). In traditional Jewish communities, you are expected to stand up when an elderly person enters the room. The lesson is that all elderly people have wisdom to impart, qualifying each in their own way as a Sage.

In a culture that worships youth and the novelty of newness— the new car, the newest technology—we can do well to remember the respect for our elders that Judaism teaches. Grandparents share their stories, teaching us who we are and from where we came.

In fact, having a relationship with grandparents can provide insight into our own parents. All parents have had parents, and you can learn a great deal from your family tree. The system in which your family operates is larger than just the immediate family. Often patterns are discovered that flow through many generations.

A challenge to understanding this multigenerational picture is the physical distance that often separates family members today. Grandparents used to care for children while parents worked. They often lived in the same house. However, the norm today—especially in Jewish circles—is for seniors to move to someplace warm, such as Florida or California. If we're lucky, we might visit a grandparent on holidays and during summer. As a result, the sort of relationship nurtured over time through day-to-day contact is lost. The days of going with *zeide*—Yiddish for "grandfather"—to the synagogue are over for most modern Jews.

For many, *zeide* was the repository of family history. He was the one who recalled life before the family moved to the suburbs. *Zeide* may have even remembered what life was like in "the old country." *Zeide* had wrinkled hands and a warm lap, and he knew fun songs to sing after dinner.

Who was your *zeide*, grandpa, or papa? Was he a traditional *zeide* from the old world that no longer exists, who went to synagogue to be part of a *minyan*, who had haunting memories of violence against Jews, who had a will to survive that was contagious? Was he a grandpa who liked to sit in the sun, who got on a boat and took you fishing, who seemed at peace hanging out, appearing to do nothing? Was he a papa who played cards, who met his friends at the deli, who volunteered his time at his local club?

Someday you will be the *zeide*, the grandfather to your grandchildren. How will you do it? What kind of *zeide* will you be?[20]

BECOMING OUR OWN MAN

We know that the path to manhood begins by identifying with our fathers beyond the fantasies of childhood. It means honoring them, even if we do not believe we will ever be half the men they are—even if they disappointed us, to our lasting hurt. In each man there is a questing boy in search of a wise old man, and many times the mentors we seek are alternate or surrogate fathers whom we need to show us the way. Even when we have been blessed with wonderful father figures, we still bring the unfinished business of our boyhood with us as we grow from stage to stage. *It is a* mitzvah *to seek to name who our fathers really were during our growing up even as we commit to honoring our parents.*

QUESTIONS FOR REFLECTION

- How you would characterize the difference between being a boy and being a man?

- The Torah presents its heroes as fallible people, often with troubled childhoods. Why do you think that is? What does this tell us about the expectations we place on ourselves?

- Much of Rabbinic literature on parenting is concerned with cultivating a child's *yetzer tov*. Who helped teach you right from wrong? How did they do so?

- Do you have a sense of the kind of man your father really is or was? What obstacles, if any, do you face in "naming your father"?

- Can you think of a time when disobeying your parents was a *mitzvah*?

- What kind of father did your father have? Does this give you more insight into the man your father is or was?

- What do you think your children would say about you as a father?

4

Growing Up and Being a Partner in Marriage

It is Friday evening, and my son has woken up late from his nap. Having slept too long, he is what my wife Julie calls "out of sorts." The phrase "out of sorts" sends chills up my spine, because it means he is liable to be hysterical at a moment's notice over the least provocation. His napkin is folded into a triangle instead of a rectangle: he cries. His cup is the blue one instead of the orange one: he cries. The only time he is not crying is when he is being held by his mother. For a young family wanting to have a peaceful dinner, the challenge of a child being "out of sorts" is very familiar.

As Julie's hands are full, she points me in the direction of the candles. It is Friday night, and it is time to begin Shabbat, our day of peace. We usher in Shabbat by lighting two lights, one for each of the commandments in the Torah to "keep" and "remember" the seventh day.

"You light them," she says.

Traditionally, the woman of the house lights the Shabbat candles, but being a modern Jewish couple, I strike the match, light the candles, and say the blessing while my wife soothes our squirming child. As a liberal rabbi, whose wife is also a liberal rabbi, we believe strongly in full equality in religion. We believe that both men and women have full access to the rituals of our tradition. We also do not believe terrible things will happen if we alter custom. We completely reject this bit of misogyny from early Rabbinic theology:

> Women die in childbirth because of three transgressions: for disregarding the laws of menstruation, for not separating dough as an offering when baking, and for failing to light the Shabbat lights. (*Mishnah Shabbat* 2:6)

I do not believe in a punishing God who strikes down women who do not light the Shabbat candles by having them die in childbirth. To our family, lighting Shabbat candles is a beautiful way of ending the workweek. With a symbol of light and warmth, we separate time so that we can pause and reflect. We carve out a moment of family togetherness for a Friday night Shabbat dinner. We take the tradition into our lives, but we deliberately leave behind some of the history of patriarchal domination. It is liberating for both women and men to include and empower both genders in all aspects of spirituality.

Some apologists for tradition claim Judaism prescribes separate but equal duties for men and women. Some say women are so much holier than men that they need not perform all the rituals men are required to perform and should therefore stay within their traditional roles.[1]

Too often, however, the roles have been separate but certainly not equal. Moreover, arguing that women should not stray from their traditional role ignores the fact that many women, although not *required* to, nonetheless *want* to participate in rituals traditionally reserved for men only. In addition, if women are so holy, why can't they perform acts of ritual leadership, such as reading from the Torah scroll on Shabbat? Liberal Judaism has set aside such boundaries.

And yet, as I lead our family in the blessing over a ritual that for thousands of years has been traditionally reserved for women, I am forced to ask some difficult questions:

- How might other men feel about performing a traditionally "feminine" ritual? Might they feel empowered or emasculated?
- Does gender matter at all? Must *equal* mean *interchangeable?*
- Is there a place for a distinctive man's role and woman's role in Judaism? In family life? In marriage?
- What about same-gender couples?
- What price have we paid for our liberation from traditional gender roles?

The one thing I am confident about is that these questions have no easy answers, and every couple building a home has to respond to them anew.

HAVE YOU READ YOUR *KETUBAH* LATELY?

The wedding couple is nervous. They gather in my office, and the *ketubah*, the Jewish marriage agreement, is laid out before them. They chose it carefully, wanting it to be a beautiful piece of art to adorn their home. Weighty objects are placed on the corners of the paper to keep it from rolling up into the shape it adopted in the cardboard tube in which it was stored. The two witnesses come forward, each of them friends. Kosher, meaning ritually acceptable, witnesses are two Jews who are not related either to the wedding couple or to each other. The *ketubah* witnesses have thus become a prime opportunity in Judaism for honoring friends.

The witnesses hold a little "cheat sheet" with their Hebrew names that I've prepared for them. It has been awhile since they had to sign their names in Hebrew; they may not have done it since Hebrew school or perhaps on a trip to Israel during college. Meanwhile the bride and groom look on, often holding hands, sometimes clutching each other tightly as the realization of what is happening sinks in. Finally, the *ketubah* is read aloud.

As meaningful as the *ketubah* is, with all of its elegant calligraphy, it is what cannot be spelled out in black-and-white where the real adventure of marriage lies. It is in the spaces between the letters, in the unknown, that lies the greatest potential for both joy and sorrow. There is no way to write down all the duties a person takes on as a partner in marriage. They cannot be spelled out entirely in advance so that one can go down the list and check them off. Yet each of the two partners desperately wants to live up to their responsibilities to their spouse.

When it comes to choosing a *ketubah*, I take a very liberal perspective. When I meet with couples prior to their wedding, I caution them: "Do not get a traditional *ketubah* in Aramaic." Why not? they ask. Why not get the most time-honored *ketubah* available? The reason is that the traditional *ketubah* comes from a time in history when men ruled society and women where often treated as chattel. In modern times, "progressive," "liberal," and "modern" texts are now available.

The gathered listeners at the *ketubah* ceremony may not know it, but the words of a contemporary *ketubah* are radically different from the words of a *ketubah* from the past. According to one's frame of reference and opinion, the tradition has either been broken or renewed. In tracking the changes made to the *ketubah*, especially in the last century, one can see how much what is expected of a man in marriage has changed.

For thousands of years, marriage looked something like this: In a match arranged by parents, a girl moved from the protection of her father's house to the protection of her husband's. The man (or boy) proposed to the girl, even though the decision to propose was usually made by the parents, and the boy had little choice in the matter. Similarly, she consented, frequently (though unofficially) under duress.

In accordance with Jewish rites, the man gave her something of value that she accepted, which traditionally became a ring. The couple moved into their home together, supplied with a dowry by the bride's father, and on their first time alone consummated the marriage and made it binding legally. If a Jewish man wanted to divorce his wife, he could do so by handing her a document called a *get*. She could not legally divorce him; it was a one-way procedure.

In response to these conditions, Rabbi Shimon ben Shetach established the beginnings of a *ketubah,* a written document that was prescribed by the Sages to protect a woman in case of divorce. If a man divorced his wife, he would have to "pay her *ketubah,*" that is, an agreed upon sum so that she would not be left destitute. This sum was two hundred *zuz* (a biblical coin) if she was a virgin at the time of marriage and one hundred if she was not, as in the case of a widow or divorcee. In addition, he would have to return an additional one hundred *zuz* of her dowry and another one hundred *zuz* as an additional gift. The total thus comes to four hundred *zuz* for a new bride. (If the well-known Passover ditty about buying a kid for two *zuzim* has any truth in it, this means a Jewish virgin was legally worth about two hundred goats, and a woman who was previously married was worth somewhat less.) These funds were guaranteed by a lien on "the best of his property" even to "the shirt off his back."[2] In other words, the original *ketubah* was a prenuptial agreement to protect a woman from poverty based upon ancient assessments of value in a patriarchal world. Today, the *ketubah* has no legal force in a civil court, yet the signing of a *ketubah* is still a religious requirement for Jewish marriage.

In its time, the traditional *ketubah* was a revolutionary document. Rather than be treated as chattel, it gave women the status of personhood. It also took an event that could have been an impulsive act and gave it grounding in familial responsibility. It provided a written record of a sacred occasion, tying a moment of holiness to a time and place.

As bold a move as this was two thousand years ago in the advancement of women's rights and the marking of sacred relationships, we have, hopefully, moved far beyond such modest standards today. As a product of its time, the *ketubah* also assumes roles that both men and women are to fulfill. Specifically, the traditional *ketubah* states on behalf of the man:

> I will work for you, honor, provide for, and support you, in
> accordance with the practice of Jewish husbands, who work

for their wives, honor, provide for, and support them with integrity.

In addition, the man had to provide "food, clothing, and other necessary benefits" and pledge to live with his wife "in accordance with the requirements prescribed for each husband."

The husband's role was thus defined primarily as a provider of physical goods. The man's job was to supply the necessities of life: food, clothing, and shelter. One of the "necessary benefits" was also understood to mean sex on a regular basis. The man was a giver of financial support to his dependents, and he was to do so with honor and respect.

FROM "ME" TO "WE"

For many Jews who aspire to live their life according to Jewish law, a traditional *ketubah* is essential. It helps define the foundation of Jewish status and identity. For this reason, some rabbis will insist on only having a traditional *ketubah*, and others will ask that a couple have a traditional *ketubah* and then use a second, more liberal one as part of the wedding ceremony.

Many, however, desire a simple statement of the sacred covenant of their relationship for their *ketubah*, tying them to Jewish tradition and values. For these couples, the traditional *ketubah* can be abandoned altogether in exchange for a beautiful declaration in Hebrew and in English that speaks to the integrity, sacredness, and commitment of their marriage.

Compare the traditional *ketubah* text with this popular liberal version:

> The groom _____ says to the bride: With this
>   *(name)*
> ring you are consecrated unto me as my wife according to
> the tradition of Moses and the Jewish people. I shall treasure
> you, nourish you, support you, and respect you as Jewish
> men have devoted themselves to their wives with integrity.

The bride _____ says to the groom: With
               (name)
this ring you are consecrated unto me as my husband according to the tradition of Moses and the Jewish people. I
shall treasure you, nourish you, support you, and respect
you as Jewish women have devoted themselves to their husbands with integrity.

We promise to try to be ever open to one another
while cherishing each other's uniqueness, to comfort and
challenge each other through life's sorrow and joy, to share
our insight and intuition with one another, and above all to
do everything within our power to permit each of us to become the persons we are yet to be.

We also pledge to establish a home open to the spiritual potential in all life; a home wherein the flow of the
seasons and the passages of life are celebrated through
the symbols of our Jewish heritage; a home filled with reverence for learning, loving, and generosity; a home
wherein ancient melody, candles, and wine sanctify the
table; a home joined ever more closely to the community
of Israel. This marriage has been authorized by the civil
authorities of _____. It is valid and
                        (state/country)
binding.³

In this liberal text, the original *ketubah*, conceived as a prenuptial
agreement, has been completely obliterated. Any trace of the *ketubah*
as a legal document is completely gone. Instead, there is a mutual
and equal statement of spiritual values. Rather than defining a
man's role in his obligations to his wife, the text states identical obligations of a man to his wife and a wife to her husband. This then
leads to a joint statement in the name of the couple, using the pronoun "we." Instead of a man providing food, clothing, shelter, and
sex for procreation, the focus is on joint emotional support,
growth, and religious observance through time. Such a sweeping
and essential change in the understanding of the basic underpin-
nings of a marriage is nothing less than radical.

This transformation of the *ketubah* eliminates all gender differences. Yet we are inescapably male and female. If Jewish married men are no longer defined as being providers, then what are our responsibilities?

WHAT WE THOUGHT WE WERE GETTING INTO WHEN WE GOT MARRIED

Women had to become equal partners with men for such changes to take place in our understanding of marriage. It is sometimes forgotten that the movement for gender equality is a relatively recent phenomenon. (American women did not win the right to vote in federal elections until 1920, when the Nineteenth Amendment to the Constitution was passed.) As Jewish life does not occur in a vacuum, the Jewish understanding of marriage, and a man's role in it, has changed as society itself transformed.

For many couples, the traditional marriage roles of the woman as homemaker and the man as breadwinner and provider continue to be intensely gratifying. As the original *ketubah* assumes, men and women have different roles to play in the tasks of love and marriage, each with different strengths and weaknesses that often complement each other. Researcher Judith S. Wallerstein explains the assumptions she held growing up:

> The kind of marriage we all expected to have was a traditional one, in which husband and wife have different roles and responsibilities, separate spheres of operation. Although the spheres overlap, they constitute distinct psychological and social realms. In the idealized form of the older model of traditional marriage, the man's primary job and self-definition is to provide for the economic well-being, protection, and stability of his family. The woman's job and self-definition is to care for her husband and children and to create a comfortable home that nourishes everyone, particularly her husband, who comes home each evening

drained by the demands of his job. The home that the
woman creates and the man supports is the haven where
the children are raised.[4]

There are many attractions and assumptions that bring a man into
a traditional marriage. In this type of marriage, life is well-ordered.
Family comes first, and what this kind of man wants most is his
wife's care and admiration. More than romance or passion, he
needs her gentleness and respect. In response, she expects to take
care of him and that his professional work will always take priority
over hers. He also assumes that she enjoys raising children and has
more talent in this area than he does.[5] And there is built-in "alone
time" as well: she goes off-duty when the kids are at school or at a
weekend activity, and he can relax when he comes home from
work.

The traditional marriage has a long history in Judaism. In the
Talmud, a woman is often called a man's *bayit*, his home. House
and wife are considered the same thing and are referred to using
the same word.[6]

The feminist movement, both in the larger society and within
Judaism, allowed women to become more prominent in the public
sphere. Feminists refused to be identified by patriarchal assumptions and fought for equality. This movement also challenged men
to redefine themselves. Men have been forced to think about their
roles at work and at home differently. Together, men and women
deliberately sought a new model of marriage to pursue.

Wallerstein has called this type of marriage, unknown in the
1950s, "companionate" marriage.[7] According to Wallerstein, a
common expectation of people with this type of marriage is that
"men and women are equal partners in all spheres of life and that
their roles, including those of marriage, are completely interchangeable.... [These couples] are actively rejecting the models
[of marriage] they experienced as children and those they see in
society at large."[8] Out of a sense of trying "to create together something joyful, new, and egalitarian," younger men are rewarded by

being closer to their children from infancy on.[9] The result is a marriage with less distinct relationship roles, more freedom, but also more uncertainty.

"A Helper to Match Him"

But does companionate marriage have a basis in Judaism?

One can find a precedent in the Jewish wedding liturgy. In the Jewish wedding ceremony, bride and groom are compared to none other than Adam and Eve. In the seven wedding blessings, we pray that "these loving companions are as happy as the joy that was felt in the Garden of Eden." The reason for this analogy can be discovered by reading the biblical story itself.

In the story of creation in the book of Genesis, God announces, "It is not good for man to be alone; I will make a helper to match him" (Genesis 2:18). God then brings all the animals and birds to Adam, and Adam gives each one a name. Naming, however, is a relationship of a subject to an object. Adam looks at each thing as an *it*. He has trouble finding anything he can relate *to*.

Adam names all the other living creatures in the world, but he does not find his match, a partner in a relationship. When God sees this, in the first act of anesthesia before surgery, God causes Adam to fall asleep. The Torah then says that God "took one of his ribs" (Genesis 2:21) and made it into a woman. When Adam wakes up, he discovers his true partner. This is someone to whom he can relate. He says:

> This one at last
> is bone of my bones
> and flesh of my flesh.
> This one shall be called Woman,
> for from man was she taken. (Genesis 2:23)

Humankind's core dilemma seems to be loneliness. Adam searches for companionship among the rest of God's creatures. He is automatically excluded, however, in that he lives on a different level of reason than they do. He can name them, but he cannot relate to them. He can talk, but they cannot speak back. There is no dialogue in his life. A dog is not a man's best friend.

The traditional translation has it that Eve was fashioned from Adam's rib, but Jewish commentary points out that the Hebrew wording literally means she was taken from his "side." Jewish tradition elaborates on this to explain that, instead of Eve being taken from a rib, the original human being was split down the middle into two sides, male and female. God created each in the divine image and then divided them equally.

It is for this reason that each wedding couple is compared to Adam and Eve. These two were originally one, halves of the same whole. The idea that the original human contained both masculine and feminine traits and had to be split down the middle implies a sense of affinity, balance, and mutuality.

A companionate-style marriage is similar; it is a view of men and women as equal and balanced. An interpretation from the tenth-century Jewish commentator Rabbi Solomon ben Isaac (better known as Rashi) adds to this sense of equality. The Torah says that the creation of a companion was to make "a helper to match him" (Genesis 2:18). Rashi states, "If he is worthy, she shall be a help to him; if he is unworthy, she shall be a match to him to challenge him."[10]

There is Jewish tradition and precedent to support the idea that men and women are meant to be equal partners. They are supposed to support each other in times of trial, but also to challenge each other when they fail to live up to their potential. How we define this equality, and the roles that each person plays, is up to us.

The payoff of a companionate style of marriage is that each partner is free to share in the joys of pursuing his or her personal hopes and dreams as well as the elation of raising children. The couple shares everything: the economic stress, the cooking and cleaning, the paycheck, the child rearing, and the fulfillment of a career. Whereas in a traditional marriage, he gives her support and protection in exchange for her nourishment and care, companionate marriages have much more overlap. They require a very high degree of self-confidence, trust, and a sense of fairness.

It also seems to me to be a large part of what Jewish men want out of a marriage today, even if they do not always realize it.

Acknowledging Our History of Patriarchal Domination

I acknowledge that the Torah also says that after Adam and Eve sinned, God punishes Eve by giving her painful childbirth and by declaring that "your urge shall be for your husband, and he shall rule over you" (Genesis 3:16). It is important to understand that this exists only after they have sinned and were expelled from the Garden. Such inequality was not God's original intent. The traditional seven wedding blessings specifically reference man and woman *in the Garden of Eden* as the ideal to which each should aspire.

Even if this inequality is not the intended ideal, history made it the norm. Men have historically asserted control, and women are praised in traditional literature for being obedient. One Hebrew word for "husband" is *ba'al*, which is synonymous with "owner." For this reason, contemporary Israeli Hebrew instead uses the word *ish*, simply meaning "man." Men's need to "govern" in the Bible is modified by the previous clause that a woman's desire should be for her man, to which we might add, and for him alone. The male need to control is born out of anxiety.[11] This feeling obviously violates the last of the Ten Commandments, applicable to both men and women, that we are not to covet.

The need to control a woman and her passions, to contain and dominate her, has caused extreme harm to both men and women. In the language of another liberation movement, both the oppressor and the oppressed need to be liberated from bondage.[12]

Both Adam and Eve are punished by Eve's subjugation. In fact, a man's strength is tested not by how much control he has over his partner but by his lack of a need for control. True strength is found in the faith and trust of a relationship, not in domination.

The test today is to demonstrate our masculinity without the need to command our partner in marriage. Men need to release patriarchy and let it recede into the past. We must keep in the forefront of our minds that Eden was the ideal in which our partner is "bone of my bones, and flesh of my flesh" (Genesis 2:23).

A Balancing Act

Several years ago, two people we will call Mitchell and Sharon met as graduate students. They originally met online and discovered that one was attending Georgetown Law School and the other George Washington University Law School, practically around the corner from each other in Washington, D.C. They met for coffee, and Sharon convinced Mitchell to join her coed volleyball team. Mitchell was not particularly comfortable as an athlete, but he was willing to fake it to spend more time with Sharon.

It did not take long before they were seeing each other every day, and a love affair grew. On the anniversary of their first date, Mitchell took Sharon to a very nice restaurant, and he asked Sharon to marry him. She happily agreed, but they also agreed to have their wedding after they both graduated.

Mitchell and Sharon began meeting with a rabbi for premarital counseling, and before long the first major challenge of their relationship arose. Each wanted to engage in a national search for their first job. As they were going to each graduate from prestigious law schools, they felt confident that they might each get offered a great opportunity. But these could easily be in different parts of the country. Whose career would take the lead?

They decided to each go on their interviews and see what would happen. In the end, Sharon was offered a job at a great law firm in Washington, and Mitchell, putting his ego aside, halted his interview process and started an exclusively local search. They married, studied and passed the bar, and started new jobs, all in a short matter of months.

"It was a very difficult time," Mitchell reflects. "It was a balancing act of what was important for each person. We are both ambitious people, but our relationship came first. We love each other very much."

Today, Mitchell and Sharon each work full-time. Mitchell enjoys his job working for a law firm that deals with telecommunications. While it was not his first choice, he feels satisfied.

They have two children. If a child awakes during the night, they take turns getting out of bed to soothe the child back to sleep. In the morning, Mitchell drops the kids off at a day care center at a large Conservative synagogue near their home, and Sharon picks them up at the end of the day. Sharon says, "We make it work. It is wonderful that I have a partner who enables me to be the kind of woman and have the kind of career that I want. As I explained to my mom when we became engaged, I was marrying a real mensch."

Recently, their first child had her third birthday. They decided to have a party at their house. Mitchell made all of the party games, and Sharon went shopping for all of the food and decorations. At the party, Mitchell taught all of the invited kids how to go "fishing" using wooden sticks and string with magnets tied to the ends, dipping them into a plastic tub of paper fish with paper clips on them. He happily spent an exhausting day running back and forth to the barbecue and holding the video camera. Sharon blew a whistle to announce when the kids were supposed to go from one activity to another, gave out party favors, and sliced cake. "We make a good team," Mitchell said.

Mitchell and Sharon spend a great deal of time thinking about their marriage. In no way is Sharon defined solely as Mitchell's *bayit*; she is certainly his "match." They value the sense of equality between them. They share everything, from the challenges of raising their children to late-night discussions about their careers. Their marriage requires a great deal of effort and trust.

Not unlike Adam in Genesis, Mitchell wanted someone to whom he could relate. "I wouldn't want to be married to a woman who didn't work the way I do. I want someone to share what I go through every day."

Breadwinner Anxiety

We might wonder what would happen to Mitchell and Sharon's marriage if their careers and child-rearing duties were not equally balanced. What happens if everything is not so evenhanded?

A man we will call Aaron confesses that he "simply couldn't handle" his relationship with his wife after she became the primary financial provider. Their marriage ended in divorce.

"It's not that we didn't like being with each other," Aaron explains. "It was that my wife was also my boss for a time. And even when she no longer was, it still felt that way. I know plenty of men whose wives work for them, but not the other way around. I couldn't take it anymore."

Aaron admits that there were other problems in the marriage. The main source of tension came from his idealistic vision of the future. "We met at work. When we met, we were both on the same level at the company. We went on business trips together. It was fun.

"Then she was promoted to be a vice president. We each said that it didn't matter, that we loved each other no matter what. We got married, with a whole big expensive wedding.

"But it just wasn't working out for us with me being at a lower level than her. Even when we came home, it still felt like we were at work. I couldn't let it go, and I don't think she wanted to either. We are both very driven people.

"So I changed jobs. I found a job someplace else, and I thought that would help. But it didn't. I still felt … dominated. Overpowered. Not in control. And then she got promoted again, but in order for her to take it to the next level, we would have to move. That was the end. I wasn't moving.

"It's sad, but it's just the way it worked out."

Women face the challenge of trying to be and do everything in a companionate marriage, often trying to balance work, marriage, a personal life, and being the primary caretaker of children. Men face the task of learning to share power and responsibility in a relationship in which they historically had control.

You might think most men would feel relief having a partner whose income matched or exceeded their own, thereby reducing the pressure on them to provide. This does not seem to be the case. One sociologist points out that men today increasingly suffer from what's been dubbed "breadwinner anxiety," where men become anxious over dependency on a wife's salary rather than relieved by the support.[13] Being a "helper to match him," or even surpass him, is not always welcome.

Completely abandoning traditional gender roles in marriage is very difficult and rare. In this respect, Mitchell and Sharon are unusual. Most couples seem to create a compromise between traditional expectations and a contemporary sense of fairness. As much as modern partners in marriage strive for equality, statistically women still tend to do more housework than men, and men are more likely to spend more time at work. (Recently, the U.S. Department of Labor determined that men spend 8.3 hours a day at work compared to 7.7 for women; women average about an hour more of housework a day than men.)[14] But the differences are deeper than dividing up chores; whether because of biology or societal pressure, psychologists tell us that men still seem to put a higher premium on autonomy than do women, and women still seem to value intimacy to a greater degree.[15] Even in the most modern of marriages, there still seem to be some traditional differences that run along gender lines, perhaps only less so than in previous generations. Traditional or not, every marriage is a compromise. Each couple must seek out its own healthiest path with integrity.

Aaron's story ought to make men ask some sharply focused questions:

- Are we really comfortable if our spouse makes more money than we do?
- Are we truly willing to leave a job and move to further her career?
- Can we be content staying home and raising children, being alone during a good part of the day?

When God split Adam and Eve into their two separate selves, they became two individuals. No marriage is going to end our separateness or entirely fill our personal sense of being essentially alone in the world.

The self-confidence, trust, and fairness that a companionate marriage requires are difficult to maintain. The work and compromise that it takes as two people share life's journey requires an ongoing effort, as well as a certain amount of luck. To enter into a covenant with another means remaining open to all possibilities and realities.

One of these realities is that sometimes men have different needs than women. The centuries-old male need, made explicit in traditional Judaism, to provide, protect, and take care of another is very strong and legitimate. If that need is not met, many men will not feel whole.

Marrying to fulfill someone else's expectations—whether they be traditional ones of breadwinner and homemaker, or modern ones of equality—without taking into account one's own true feelings undermines any marriage contract, no matter how elegant the words of the *ketubah*. Jewish men, like all men, need to be true to themselves in their individuality when making sacred promises with a partner.

MASCULINITY, FEMININITY, AND JEWISH SACRED WRITING

In his book *Taking Sex Differences Seriously*, Dr. Steven E. Rhoads points out that biology still matters. This relates to more than the fact that men have ten times the amount of testosterone than women have; positron emission tomography (PET) scans show the map of a woman's brain as more "networked" and a man's as more "compartmentalized" with more single-minded focus.[16] This different brain pattern translates into different behaviors and approaches to challenges. A host of best-selling books have highlighted natural differences in how men and women communicate, with women being more prone to empathize and men to problem-solve.[17] Rhoads also claims that "a low-testosterone male is, nonetheless, almost always masculine." Which is to say that the "girly" nerd rejected by the jocks at school is still likely to play video games at home where he gets to blow up imaginary stuff.[18]

However, other studies have shown that similarities often outweigh differences, and treating men and women as if they are two different species is overblown.[19] Rather than men being "from Mars" and women being "from Venus," as one popular book states,[20] both men and women are "from Earth."[21] We have many of the same hopes and fears, and the challenges of life affect us both indiscriminately.

We are thus faced with a paradox: while men and women are biologically distinct, each has the hormones of the other, and each has masculine and feminine aspects to their personality. Masculinity and femininity are therefore defined as a matter of emphasis and tendencies rather than as wholly separate qualities. Carl Jung insisted that each male has an *anima*, an internalized feminine aspect, and every woman has an *animus*, an internalized masculine aspect.[22] The Chinese speak of yin and yang, and in many other cultures we find that what is masculine and feminine is both distinctive and within each person, male and female. In Judaism, this understanding of the masculine and feminine (and the paradox that they are always combined within each person) is evident in the sacred writings of the Rabbis.

In the Talmud, God is depicted as struggling with how to treat God's most troublesome creation, humanity. On the one hand, God can act with an attribute of judgment by enforcing rules and drawing boundaries. On the other, God loves us and treats us with compassion. The Hebrew word for "compassion" is *rachamim*, which shares the same origin as "womb." It is for this reason, it has been argued, that for the Talmudic Rabbis, the tendency to judge and enforce is predominantly male, while the tendency to care and be empathetic is predominately female.[23]

However, biblical examples abound in which men and women can be both forceful in their power and nurturing in their compassion. Moses, for instance, not only kills an Egyptian who is beating an Israelite slave (thus acting on his attribute of judgment), he also is told to lead the Israelites and "carry them in your bosom as a nurse carries an infant" (Numbers 11:12).

Similarly, Jewish legend demonizes the extremes of masculinity and femininity. In the Garden of Eden, Eve is seduced by a snake, a phallic image that is all about violating boundaries and pursuing desires. The snake is, as one writer calls him, "pure penis."[24] On the opposite end of the spectrum, Jewish folklore tells us of Lilith, a mythological female demon spurned by Adam in favor of Eve. Lilith is reputed to cause crib death and kill young men. In between these poles represented by the snake and Lilith are Adam and Eve, human in their shared sexual intimacy.[25] Being purely masculine and feminine is inhuman, the Rabbis seem to be telling us. It also leads to violence. Masculinity and femininity need to be balanced and mixed with each other for there to be life.

BEING A COMPLETE "ADAM"

In no other place in Judaism, however, do the concepts of masculine and feminine play a more important role than in Jewish mysticism, called kabbalah. Building off of the Sages' imagery, kabbalah takes the qualities of male and female in extraordinary and unprecedented directions. Masculinity and femininity become tools the kabbalists use to understand God, the world, and themselves.

The Talmud states that a man without a wife is not whole, for it says in Genesis that when God created Adam, God made male and female (Babylonian Talmud, *Yevamot* 63a). In other words, a man cannot be a complete "Adam" without both male and female in his life. Jewish mystics of later centuries read this comment in the Talmud hyper-literally—that no person is complete without having both masculine and feminine aspects. Each person has a masculine and a feminine side, and it is important to channel the qualities of each at appropriate times.

The twelfth-century book central to Jewish mysticism, the *Zohar*, contains the following passage on the phrase "In the image of God, male and female God created them" (Genesis 1:27):

"Male and female He created them"
to make known the Glory on high,
the mystery of faith.
Out of this mystery, Adam was created....

From here we learn:
Any image that does not embrace male and female
is not a high and true image....

The Blessed Holy One does not place His abode
in any place where male and female are not found together....
A human being is only called Adam
when male and female are as one.[26]

The *Zohar* states that because Adam was made in God's image and was made with both masculine and feminine sides, God's image is both male and female and is incomplete without both. In fact, when having to initiate someone into Jewish mystical circles, kabbalists of the Middle Ages looked for traits that indicated the student's masculine and feminine aspects were in balance so that "the Blessed Holy One" could "place His abode" in the person. They did this through palm reading, looking at the right hand for men and the left hand for women.[27]

More significant than ancient initiation rites is the basic idea that both primordial Adam and even God are made of both male and female. According to Jewish mystics, human beings, being made in God's image, reflect aspects of the Divine. The fact that the original Adam was both masculine and feminine means to the kabbalists that God is made of both male and female. Furthermore, as God is everywhere and pervades existence, the masculine and feminine are also to be found throughout creation. Human beings are considered a microcosm of the universe, a "little world" (*Tanchuma Pekudei* 3), and masculine and feminine aspects are to be found not only within human beings but also in heaven and earth.

To illustrate this idea, the early kabbalists envisioned a system of *sefirot*, or divine features. In kabbalistic writing, these features are used to represent everything from God's qualities and biblical characters, to degrees of revelation and names for the Divine. The *sefirot* are thus a mystical picture of how the kabbalists thought God relates to the world and to human beings. The metaphorical imagery is strikingly sexual.

Among the *sefirot*, the masculine aspects of God are understood to be transcendent, that is, of the upper worlds, and the feminine are believed to be immanent, or here on earth among us. The Hebrew name for the masculine in kabbalistic terminology is *Tiferet*, or "the Righteous One." He is the pillar that can connect heaven and earth. The feminine is termed *Shekhinah*, a feminine word for God's presence. The upper *Tiferet* and the lower *Shekhinah* are meant to be in balance and united, masculinity being outgoing and expansive, and femininity channeling and leading. If the *sefirot* are not in balance, masculinity is unrestrained, and femininity is abandoned or in exile. The task of the mystic is to stimulate union of the masculine and the feminine through the performance of *mitzvot*, God's commandments.[28] The thirteenth-century mystic Joseph Gikatilla spells out the power of humanity to unite male and female and bring harmony to the world through their actions:

The Righteous One stands gazing out at humanity. When he sees human beings engaged in Torah and mitsvot, seeking to refine themselves, to conduct themselves in purity, then the Righteous One expands, filling himself with all kinds of flowing emanation from above, to pour into Shekhina, the divine presence, in order to reward those purifying themselves, those cleaving to Torah and mitsvot. Thus, the entire world is blessed by those righteous humans, and Shekhinah is likewise blessed through them.

But if, God forbid, humans defile themselves by distancing themselves from Torah and mitsvot, by perpetrating evil, injustice, and violence, then the Righteous One stands to gaze at what they have done. When he sees, he gathers and contracts himself, ascending higher and higher. Then the flow of all the channels ceases, and Shekhina is left dry and empty, lacking all good.[29]

For the mystics, masculine and feminine aspects hold cosmic significance. The early kabbalists felt they were in exile and strove to create harmony. They chose to illustrate these efforts through sexual imagery between male and female. A righteous person, through study and deeds, can bring harmony between male and female to the world, and even to the Divine.

Yet the kabbalists were also insistent that they were not dualists. God may incorporate masculine and feminine aspects within the Divine, but God also transcends them. Masculinity and femininity are thus human images that the mystics admitted they employed to point to a higher truth. The kabbalists insisted that God is one, without any duality, but human sexual union is a valuable metaphor to understand the ecstatic feeling of God's unity. Psychologists would call these metaphors projections, but for mystics they were revelations of Divine truths.

> Everything I created, I made in pairs: heaven and earth, the sun and the moon, Adam and Eve, this world and the world-to-come. I, however, am gloriously one, without comparison in the world. (Deuteronomy Rabbah 2:31)

We cannot achieve the unity or harmony that is the sole province of God, but the kabbalists would still teach that we must strive for balance. If we take the metaphor that each human being is a microcosm of the universe seriously, then just as nature needs balance so does human nature. The masculine and the feminine within must be brought into balance, and a relationship with another must be balanced as well.

It is also instructive to compare the definitions of what is masculine and feminine according to the kabbalists versus what we assume in the Western world. As previously noted, Western thinking often defines being masculine as being forceful and aggressive, and being feminine as being receptive and passive. Kabbalistic imagery, however, illustrates a different scenario. On the feminine side of the *sefirot*, we find the traits of understanding, power, and splendor. On the masculine side, we find wisdom, loving-kindness, and endurance. The feminine power is understood to be guiding and directing. Masculinity is seen in bestowing grace. In this scenario, women are anything but passive, and men are passionate in their ability to feel.

HOLY SEX!

It is important to note that according to the *ketubah*, the "necessary benefits" a man owed his wife included sex, considered to be a woman's conjugal right. This was mostly so that she could conceive and bear children, but even if this was not possible, sex was understood by the Sages to be a healthy part of any loving relationship.[30] The Talmud goes so far to prescribe how often a man should have sex with his partner, which varies according to his occupation and whether he is required to travel and for how long:

> The obligation as it is understood in the Torah is that for idle men, every day. For workers, twice a week. For donkey drivers, once a week. For camel drivers, once a month. For sailors, once every six months. (*Mishnah Ketubot* 5:6)

Rabbinic wisdom: it pays to be idle.

Sex, from the Sages' point of view, was a wonderful part of a relationship to be enjoyed as a gift from God. In fact, married partners having sex on the Sabbath is considered the ideal. The philosopher Moses Maimonides wrote, "It is the practice of the disciples of the wise to have conjugal relations each Friday night" (*Mishneh Torah, Hilchot Ishut* 14:1).[31] Such intimacy was deemed to be more than just the pursuit of pleasure; it was considered holy.

In the thirteenth-century Hebrew manuscript *Iggeret Hakodesh* ("The Holy Letter"), we find not only the Rabbis' positive view of sex but also how a man should conduct himself with his partner. The values of love, honesty, health, joy, respect, and modesty pervade the text. Never is a man to be domineering, disloyal, or disrespectful.

> Know that the sexual intercourse of man with his wife is holy and pure when done properly, in the proper time and with the proper intention. No one should think that sexual intercourse is ugly and loathsome, God forbid![32]

Lewdness in any fashion is not in harmony with Jewish values. It is also against Jewish law to have sex without another's consent. Another source tells us that sex is never to be used as a weapon, either physically or emotionally:

> [A man] should not carry his jealousy of [his wife] beyond reason, nor should he compel her to have intercourse with him against her will. Rather, he should do it only with her consent, accompanied by pleasant discourse and enjoy-

ment. [Likewise,] she should not deny herself to her husband merely in order to torment him. (*Mishneh Torah, Hilchot Ishut* 15:17–18)[33]

Sexual partners are supposed to respect each other's feelings. As the ultimate act of intimacy, it is an extraordinary way of honoring and caring for another. According to *Iggeret Hakodesh*, before there is to be a meeting of bodies there should first be a meeting of minds:

> When engaging in the sex act, you must begin by speaking to her in a manner that will draw her heart to you, calm her spirits, and make her happy. Thus your minds will be bound upon one another, and your intentions will unite with hers.[34]

In a culture that shows men being "manly" by aggressively dominating their partners sexually, the Jewish "uniting of intentions" and "calming spirits" shows another way. Sex is more than ogling at a strip club or downloading pornography, two activities dominated almost exclusively by men. Nothing could be further from how the Rabbis understood the duty of a real man. When done properly, sex is a spiritual connection between two loving people.

Maintaining this connection is not necessarily easy. If we think of sex as an act of passion, then working full-time and coming home exhausted at the end of the day can drain away our sexual drive. Add to this the challenge of protecting our privacy against children, and passionate moments can become fewer and farther between.

Iggeret Hakodesh seems more about nurturing a sexual relationship over time than trying to fit in moments of desire. A spiritual sexual relationship is much more about intimacy than passion. The familiar touch brings joy and comfort, and closeness and understanding build trust. As we grow older and our needs and desires change, "minds bound together" takes on a deeper meaning.

Gender Does and Does Not Matter

So does gender matter or doesn't it?

The answer appears to be yes and no. Gender still matters in that men and women have different biological and social tendencies. It matters in how we communicate, what we naturally feel first, and what we have been conditioned to think of as important. Gender matters in how we complement another as a partner, with our strengths and our weaknesses. Our initial instincts may start from different places, but that does not need to be where we end up. As psychologist Brad E. Sachs, director of the Father Center in Columbia, Maryland, has put it, we need to "accept gender differences," and we can "feel free to escape them."[35]

Regardless of gender, each individual is a person with hopes and dreams. Each individual has needs, including not only companionship but also privacy, not only security but also encouragement to risk, not only helping another to grow but also growing him- or herself. Perhaps this is what is meant when the Torah states that both men and women were created in God's image: there is God-given worth simply in being human.

There are many ways to be happily married. How a couple meets the challenges of marriage seems less important than that the tasks of marriage are in fact met. These are tasks—tasks that require effort and deliberate actions. In going on life's journey, it means both people deciding to go a certain way together despite other options.

Perhaps the secret to happiness in marriage is not whether one pursues a traditional, companionate, or some kind of hybrid marriage, but rather whether or not each person's goals and needs are met. And all marriages are imperfect. Adam and Eve will forever reach toward each other, but that does not mean that they will ever be reunited the way they once were. Equal, it seems, does *not* mean interchangeable. Marriage requires change and accommodation in sharing life's road. We may consciously or unconsciously choose a certain approach to being married that suits us best, but that still means we have hard work to do.

- Can a marriage create time and space for both togetherness and individuality?
- Can it be a safe place for anger, conflict, and crises?
- Can it be a bond for sexuality, laughter, and productivity?
- Can each partner nurture their own and each other's self-esteem, dreams, and ideals?[36]

Same-Gender Couples

I believe that if one defines a happy marriage in terms of fulfilling tasks, that is, meeting personal goals and dreams, then this applies to same-gender couples just as much as to male and female couples. Gender matters a great deal in defining who we are and who we choose as a partner, but it does not limit our potential for happiness. Two men or two women can be equally fulfilled and loved as one man and one woman.

If we are going to take manhood seriously, then including the gay community as a group of men is a must. Serious manhood comes with serious covenantal commitment, which for Judaism means marriage.

Some may argue that homosexuality is banned in the Torah in Leviticus chapter 18, but the Torah also asks us to execute witches and stone people who pick up sticks on Shabbat. Unless we want to be fundamentalists, we cannot insist on understanding one passage of our Bible literally and relying upon interpretation to understand another when convenient.

Some argue that marriage has traditionally always been between one man and one woman, and we ought not change this hallowed institution. But as I noted, traditional marriage values considered a woman to be chattel and the man to be her owner. Just because something is old does not necessarily make it right. Instead of these aspects of the legal tradition, we should look to the parts of the Torah that emphasize that all people are created in God's image with male and female within them. We should listen to the many times the Torah tells us to love the stranger and bring the marginalized members of society into our communities and that we should seek justice and human rights for all.

While same-gender marriage flies in the face of tradition, without ritual or legal precedent, it does so no less than the radical reinvention of the *ketubah* or other aspects of the Jewish wedding. If our focus is on the idea that each person has inherent worth and each individual has tasks that they need as a partner to fulfill, then same-gender marriage is a natural extension of this transformation of the institution. Gender matters on a personal level, but the end result of two people, whatever the gender of those people might be, fulfilling their covenantal responsibilities is the same. Marriage demands mature behavior from two individuals, and the evolution of this institution to include same-gender couples can only bring a blessing to our community in the responsible standards it upholds.

At the time of this writing, some states in America are advocating for the legal recognition of same-gender marriage, and there is an equally forceful movement against it. The liberal denominations of Reform and Reconstructionist Judaism have embraced this form of marriage, while it is hotly debated within the Conservative Movement, and Orthodox congregations have shunned it. A recent gay pride parade in Jerusalem produced a violent response from some ultra-Orthodox Jews.

While much more could be said about this issue, a complete history and ethical examination of being gay or lesbian is well beyond the scope of this work. It should be stated, however, that gay Jewish men who are marrying with Jewish ritual are very conscious of the fact that they are creating a new experience not only for themselves but for the Jewish people as a whole. They struggle with showing reverence for tradition while remaining authentic to who they are.

We must show special sensitivity to the fact that being gay is far from new and that the desire of gay men and women to openly announce and celebrate their love to family, friends, and the community at large is no different than the desire of a heterosexual couple. Gay people continue to suffer discrimination, are the victims of crimes of hate, and often feel shame in going against other people's expectations. Too often, they feel rejection at the hands of the people who are supposed to love them the most.

To sanctify a relationship between two Jewish men under a *chuppah*, a wedding canopy, with a cup of wine does more than recognize the legitimacy of a union created by God. It is also a repudiation of prejudice and oppression and an affirmation of human rights. It brings the support of community into the private lives of two people who love each other. It also affirms that we reinvent traditional practices as human beings struggle to morally progress and evolve.[37]

An Important Note on Domestic Abuse

It is also incumbent upon any discussion of a man's role as a marriage partner to strongly condemn any form of domestic abuse— physical or emotional. Violence in the home is completely contrary to Jewish values, and traditional Jewish writings have denounced such actions for centuries. In some countries where women had very low social status, Jewish authorities accepted domestic abuse as a reality they could do nothing to prevent. Others sought to deny that such abuse existed in the Jewish community, and such denial continues today. The reality is that Jewish abusers do exist and must be confronted.[38] Rabbi Joseph Karo, the author of the sixteenth-century definitive code of Jewish law known as the *Shulchan Aruch*, states that a man who beats his wife should be flogged, banned, and exiled. He even advocated cutting off such a man's hand.[39] Such pronouncements are radical in comparison to how Western society today treats abusers, but they underscore the seriousness with which such behavior was regarded.

Today, any kind of abuse between partners in marriage, or toward children or parents, is not only illegal but considered abhorrent. We must remain cognizant of the fact that we can do the most damage to others in precisely the relationships in which we are supposed to derive the most joy and be most sensitive:

> Be very careful not to hurt the feelings of your wife, for her tears are brought on easier [than others], and she is more vulnerable to hurtful gestures from you. (Babylonian Talmud, *Bava Metzia* 59a)

The Talmud also teaches:

> One who loves his wife as himself and who respects her even more than himself and teaches his children the right way should make peace in his home. (Babylonian Talmud, *Yevamot* 62b)

It is also an illusion to believe that domestic abuse results from losing one's temper on occasion or being loud when angry. Abuse is a pattern of behavior that is about *control*, not anger. Therapist Bob Gluck explains in his work with Jewish men and violence in the home:

> The abusive man tends to control others, yet he feels that it is they who control *his* life. His self-esteem is likely to be low, and he easily feels humiliated, frustrated or hurt. At the same time, this man is unlikely to identify or articulate any of these feelings. Such a man will tend to label all uncomfortable emotions "anger," but claim it is really "the other" who is angry, and not he. When not raging, he may feel depressed.[40]

Gluck finds little difference between Jewish and non-Jewish abusers; being Jewish does not make one exempt or make the problem go away. If anything, Gluck claims that his Jewish clients felt a greater sense of shame when confronted with their actions than his non-Jewish clients. While all abusers are acting upon "early role-modeling of violence combined with a lower threshold of emotional pain tolerance," Jewish men also must deal with a degree of cultural gender role conflict.[41] Jewish men may unconsciously ask themselves, "Should I act aggressively as necessary to get by in the wider world of young men, or more like a non-violent, non-aggressive 'mensch' as Jewish society might desire?"[42]

In few other contexts is emotional boyhood in grown men more dangerous. Jewish men who suspect themselves of abuse must know that their spiritual heritage demands that they seek help. Rehabilitation is possible. Twelve-step programs, such as Batterers Anonymous,[43] provide spiritual and effective solutions to men who feel they are in trouble. As substance and alcohol abuse often accompany such problems, organizations such as Jewish Alcoholics, Chemically Dependent Persons, and Significant Others (JACS) can also be a great source of help.[44]

Men are not the sole abusers, however. Women can also be guilty of abuse. Men who are being abused by women may feel unique shame in reporting their hurt as it goes against the stereotype of men being the stronger party. Nevertheless, we have a responsibility to "choose life" (Deuteronomy 30:19) and ask for help.

Because of our strong ethical history and tradition, it is incumbent upon Jewish men to recognize abuse and to act against it. An abuser can be a colleague or a family member. If you have strong suspicions about abuse by others, you must report it to the legal authorities and allow them to investigate. Jewish organizations also exist to address this problem, such as The Awareness Center, Jewish Women International, or one's local chapter of Jewish Social Services (sometimes also called Jewish Family and Children's Services).[45] Jews must not "stand by while another bleeds" (Leviticus 19:16).

You Are Holy to Me

Perhaps one of the reasons each couple at the traditional Jewish wedding is compared to Adam and Eve is because like the first couple, they also stand at the beginning of the creation of a world. Marriage is a form of creation. Each couple creates a world of feelings and insights known only by them. A relationship is in a way its own planet with boundaries and sensations. As one of the seven wedding blessings says, "May these loving companions rejoice as have Your creatures since the days of creation."[46]

During the wedding ceremony, there is typically an exchange of rings. While Jewish law dictates only that a man needs to give a woman a ring and that she give her consent, most Jewish weddings today have a double ring ceremony. Upon giving the ring, one says to the other, "Be holy to me according to the laws of Moses and Israel."

The Hebrew word for holy, *kadosh*, literally means "set apart." One person is set apart exclusively for another. This means more than the commitment to not engage in the physical act of adultery. It means that we also will emotionally open up to our partner first and foremost above any other acquaintances, relatives, or friends. Fidelity involves the entirety of our being. It means promising that this will be our most intimate relationship. *It is a* mitzvah *to endeavor to be "a matching helper" to our partners in marriage and not define ourselves solely as providers and breadwinners.*

Such setting apart, with all of the joy and support that a partnership ideally brings, also carries a higher level of responsibility to fulfill your side of the marriage covenant. It is an act of creation to constantly renew and rededicate yourself to the best that you can be.

QUESTIONS FOR REFLECTION

- If you are married, do you have a *ketubah?* Do you know what it says?
- What expectations do you have, if any, about marriage? If you have been married more than once, have your expectations changed?
- What defines an ideal marriage for you?

- To what degree do you think gender matters in your life and in your relationships?

- Kabbalah teaches that masculinity and femininity are mystical sides of each person. Do you believe this is true? How would you define masculine? Feminine?

- Which relationships in your life do you consider sacred? What does "holiness" mean to you in this context?

5

Growing Up and Being a Father

One of my earliest memories, if not the earliest, recalls being dropped off at summer camp as a small child. My father drove me to Camp Milldale in Reisterstown, Maryland. The road there was very hilly, and it cut through fields of corn and cow pastures. The dirt road through the woods opened up to the camp itself, where the youngest age groups met in a small barn. Being a Jewish day camp, the early childhood program was called *B'reishit*, the first Hebrew word of the Torah, which translates "In the beginning" (Genesis 1:1).

I remember the absolute terror I felt at being dropped off in a strange place away from my parents, what developmental psychologists today call "separation anxiety." I remember wrapping both my arms and legs around my father's leg and screaming. Dutifully, he peeled off my limbs and forced me to have what turned out to be a wonderful day at camp.

A second childhood memory has me standing on the diving board of our local pool when I was probably about five or six. On my arms were water wings, small plastic floats that enable children to bob up and down in the water. My father was in the deep end, treading water, desperately trying to get me to jump in.

I would not. There was no way I was walking off the plank. In fact, I refused to jump off the board for many years, embarrassing my parents as my peers began showing off their dives, cannonballs, and backflips.

Little could my father know, as he tiredly kicked his legs underwater time after time in the hope that I would just jump in already, that one day I would decide I really liked swimming. Not only did I jump into the water with enthusiasm, but I joined the Jewish Community Center swim team. I am sure a great deal of head scratching ensued.

I now have the joy of being a father. When I drop off my son at preschool, I have to peel his arms, and sometimes his legs, from my leg and leave him crying in his teacher's arms. I have discovered that separation anxiety is possibly much worse for parents than for children. It took a great while for my heart to stop beating fast after I "abandoned" my child to the classroom. In fact, at a certain Jewish day school with which I am familiar, there is a room where parents can go during the first week of the school year to get over the trauma of dropping off their child. "But she's screaming!" they frantically cry. The child stops crying after just a couple of minutes; parents' panic seems to last much longer.

As I noted earlier, a child's view of God is often shaped by their parents. That awareness can be overwhelming because we know we are not God. In fact, we are extraordinarily flawed, the farthest thing from perfect. The one thing of which we can be absolutely certain is that when it comes to raising a child, we have absolutely no guarantee that we know what we are doing. The minute we feel even somewhat competent, a conversation with another parent ("What do you mean you are trying to potty train at that age? That's never going to work!") is enough to make us feel completely inadequate. How dare we play God in another's life, a life that is so small and vulnerable? Shouldn't we have a degree, or at least some sort of mail-order certificate, before being allowed to take a baby home from the hospital?

For both child and parent, growth is a terrifying and exhilarating journey. As a religious Jew, I believe being a parent requires an extraordinary amount of faith. We need to have faith that our child is going to be okay, despite our inadequacies and failings. We need to have faith that our child is strong enough to grow, that God made the human spirit with enough resilience that being dropped off at camp or jumping off a diving board is not a world-stopping trauma. We need to have faith that the future will be safe enough that it is worth raising children, that there will be blessings for them to enjoy. And we need to have faith in ourselves that we have what it takes to be, if not a perfect parent, then a "good enough" parent, as psychologist Brad E. Sachs puts it.[1]

OUT OF CONTROL

Imagine how the biblical Abraham and Sarah must have felt when they finally brought their son Isaac into the world. Abraham had a previous try at fatherhood with Sarah's handmaid, Hagar, which ended in disaster. Later, long past Abraham and Sarah's years of fertility, the Bible tells us that God promises them a son. At first, the news that she will conceive makes Sarah laugh, for it seems impossible. Her bitter laughter is undoubtedly filled with disappointment as well as disbelief. However, this laughter is transformed into joy.

The Torah says that God remembers Sarah and does as was promised. She becomes pregnant, and their son is born in their old age. (Abraham is said to be one hundred years old!) At the age of eight days, Abraham circumcises their son. Sarah is given the privilege of bestowing the name Isaac (Hebrew: *Yitzchak*), meaning "laughter," for she says, "God has brought me laughter; everyone who hears will laugh with me" (Genesis 21:1–6).

In this biblical story, as in our modern stories, parenting is a mixture of anxiety and exaltation. This combination of fear and joy is especially poignant for the many contemporary fathers who are taking unprecedented steps to be engaged in child rearing. Unheard of in any earlier generation, many fathers today take "paternity leave" when a child is born. New fathers are seeking out the rewards of actively raising their children from infancy onward in growing numbers.[2] Frequently they reschedule their work hours to enable them to be part of their children's carpool or weekend activities. Many of today's fathers want closer involvement in their children's day-to-day lives. Men are also taking on the stress and worry. Just as Abraham circumcised his son when he was one hundred years old and his son had lived only eight days, fathers are required to perform acts of faith that bring out our greatest fears and hopes. In my imagination, I can hear Abraham asking himself, "Can I really do this? My father did not do this for me. What if I am a failure?" Nevertheless, Abraham, the man who set out into unknown territory entirely on faith, also voyaged into fatherhood in his old age.

Fatherhood brings hopes, dreams, and fears. Being a father is precisely the place where you surrender control, where you must admit that you do not know what the future will bring and that there are no guarantees. You do the best you can and leave the rest to God. Consider this poem, "Tallis," written by an expectant father filled with faith as he looks at his prayer shawl. The cloth will soon serve as a blanket during his son's circumcision.

> This shawl has kept my prayers warm
> Like buttered rolls in a basket
> Now the fringes split and splay out
> Readying themselves for the child
> Who will sleep in their midst
> Like a Torah dozing in the ark[3]

The Hebrew word for faith or trust is *bitachon*. It takes *bitachon* to ready oneself for the arrival of a child, faith that the delivery and all that goes with it will go well. It takes *bitachon* to believe that you can be a parent and, more pointedly, that you can and will be an active, involved father, even if your own father did not model this role for you. Perhaps your father, who loved you dearly, did not feel it was within his territory or realm of expertise to sing you to sleep or help you with homework. But that does not mean that as a contemporary Jewish man you cannot take a chance on doing something new with *bitachon* and that you will not only prove to be adequate and competent but perhaps even great.

The Talmud's Obligations on Being a Father

Even while embarking on something unprecedented, fathers can still look to ancient wisdom for guidance. The style of fathering might be new, but the emotional reality of being a father is not.

The Talmud recognizes many a father's hopes and anxieties when it lists a father's obligations to his son and, by extension, to his daughter. However, because the Talmud was written at a time when sons were raised differently than daughters, modern readers must exercise a certain flexibility when translating this text to allow for this historical context.

> The father is bound in respect of his son:
> to circumcise,
> redeem,
> teach him Torah,
> take a wife for him,
> and teach him a craft.
> Some say, to teach him to swim too.
> (Babylonian Talmud, *Kiddushin* 29a)

This passage from the Talmud lists the *mitzvot* of fatherhood in ancient times. The list may surprise some, both in what it says and in what it does not say.

Circumcising and Redeeming
It begins with the ritual requirements owed to boys; first is the act of circumcision, which symbolizes renewing the covenant. In Judaism, the symbol of the covenant is marked on precisely that part

of the body that represents procreation and the hope for future generations. It is an indelible mark of continuity.

Today, at the *b'rit milah* (literally, "covenant of circumcision"), the *mohel* or *mohelet* (circumciser) who does the actual cutting will turn to the father, moments before the surgery, to declare that he or she is acting as the father's agent unless the father would like to perform the act himself. Usually a moment of laughter follows as the father happily turns over the responsibility to someone who knows what they are doing. However, the responsibility was originally the father's.

When the cut is made, no matter what any *mohel* or *mohelet* says, it must hurt. The baby cries, but in this there is also a lesson. One of the first things you must do as a father, whether you like it or not, is accept the fact that you will cause your child pain one way or another. If you are truly doing your job, there will be other times that you cause your children discomfort, such as when you make them do things they do not want to do or of which they are fearful, when you insist on discipline and respect, and when you enable them to make their own choices and experience the hurts that follow their own mistakes.

In her groundbreaking book *The Blessing of a Skinned Knee*, teacher Wendy Mogel cautions us against coddling our children. Too often, she explains, parents are "trying to inoculate their children against the pain of life."[4] Such fathers and mothers are sometimes called "helicopter parents" because they are always hovering.[5] Even when children go away to college, they are encouraged to call home at the slightest obstacle or problem. In fact, pain is part of the process. For parents, there is *tzar gidul banim*, "the pain of raising children." But Mogel points out that it also refers to the pain experienced by our sons or daughters. Overprotecting children keeps them weak and fragile.[6]

The need to push a child forward is balanced by the second *mitzvah*, to redeem a child. Traditionally, the firstborn son of a Jewish mother was to serve in the Temple in Jerusalem. One then paid a *kohen*, a priest, to trade places with the child so that he would not have to undergo that service. For five silver coins the redemption or exchange was made. Modern Judaism preserves this custom with the ritual known as *pidyon haben*, "the redemption of the firstborn." Someone who is a *kohen*—which today means someone who traces their lineage on their father's side back to the priestly class—comes to the home or synagogue and asks, "Which would you rather do: give me the firstborn son, the first of his mother, or redeem him for five *selaim* [coins], as the Torah obligates you to do?" The father hands the money to the *kohen* and says, "I want to redeem my son, and this is his redemption money, as the Torah obligates me to do." The father than says blessings, and all join in a festive meal.

As much as the modern form of this ritual may be an excuse to have a party, the origin of the ritual was to protect a child from a task that was overwhelming and unreasonable. Just as we understand that a parent will of necessity cause their children some pain in helping them grow strong, we need to stay alert to avoid causing unnecessary pain or forcing them to take on tasks that might overwhelm them. Service in the Temple for every firstborn was understood to be excessive. Figuring out how much our child can handle at any given moment is a balancing act. You don't want to be overprotective, just as you don't want to take "tough love" too far.

Teaching Torah

The third commandment on this list of a father's responsibilities is to teach a child Torah. In fact, in Talmudic times, the father was the primary teacher of Torah in the family. There is even evidence to suggest that in communities in which there were no rabbis, fathers were the only teachers available.[7] The phenomenon of the father being the foremost teacher of Torah continued into the Middle Ages, as documents from the Cairo Genizah indicate.[8] During the Passover Seder, for instance, the role of the father at the head of the table is not just to be a leader but to be a teacher, catering to the learning style of four kinds of children: the wise, the wicked, the simple, and the one who does not even know how to ask a question.

In the small Jewish communities of Eastern Europe—the world of the shtetl—fathers tended to be stricter toward sons and more indulgent toward daughters, as the mother filled the role of the girls' disciplinarian.[9] Similarly, in Yemenite Jewish communities, sons would accompany fathers to public religious rituals; on Shabbat fathers would test sons on their week's religious instruction.[10] Today, even some of the most traditional Jewish scholars have ruled that, with women now active in the public sphere, they also must be taught Torah and be as learned as men.[11]

When a son becomes a bar mitzvah, the father traditionally says the following blessing: "Praised is the Eternal who has freed me from responsibility for this one." Many fathers laughingly say they wish parenting is completed when their sons and daughters reach thirteen, but they know parenting is far from completed at that age, if it ever is. Still, the blessing makes clear that it is the father's duty to personally see to his child's education and that, at least theoretically, a child is ready for lessons beyond the teaching of the basic commandments upon reaching thirteen.

In Western society, however, the role of the Jewish father as the personal teacher of Torah has all but disappeared. As men became increasingly enmeshed in their work and as religion became professionalized, with rabbis and cantors too often serving as the community's "professional Jews," the habit became to drop off sons and daughters at a religious school for their Jewish education. The risk of this system is that, lacking reinforcement in the home, such a limited education accomplishes very little. As with other extracurricular activities, today's Jewish child is too often expected to learn to be Jewish to the same degree that he or she learns to play piano or soccer.

Despite this trend, many synagogue schools present numerous opportunities for parental involvement. Volunteering, family learning days, and other programs invite parents to learn alongside their child. It is a chance for a father to take his historic place as a teacher of Torah in his child's life.

Fathers would likely feel more comfortable teaching their child Torah if they themselves were more Jewishly learned. Taking an adult education class, setting aside time for Shabbat, or volunteering with your child for some other kind of program is a great place to start.[12]

Recently, a father in my synagogue took issue with how I conducted a service for the families of our religious school. During this service, the children came onto the *bimah* to sing a few songs with our cantor. The attendance at this Shabbat service was very high, as many parents wanted to support their children and see them "perform." I conducted the service, leading the prayers and reading from the Torah. Afterward, this father said to me, "You know, you should have let me read from the Torah instead. I would have loved to show my boy that this isn't about just the rabbi knowing what to do, but also his father." I realized that he was absolutely right.

Taking a Wife for Him and Teaching Him a Craft

The Talmud's list continues in accordance with a child's needs as they mature. The father is obligated to arrange a match for a son and to train him in a profession so he can support himself and his own family. He needs to supply a daughter with clothes and a dowry. One commentator adds that if a father did not train his children in a profession, it was as if he taught them how to steal (Babylonian Talmud, *Kiddushin* 30b). Children will grow up and learn to fend for themselves, one way or another.

It also is incumbent upon us to have open and frank discussions with children about the most difficult issues: the "big talks" about sex and responsibility, about relationships and marriage, about finding a fulfilling career that not only pursues a dream but supports others, about the importance of family and Jewish tradition. We must both model and verbalize our thoughts and feelings. Just as important, we must be prepared to listen and even give our blessing to a path that is completely different than the one we chose for ourselves. Not offering advice or rushing to fix a child's situation but simply being present, available, and accepting can be a gift.

Perhaps the deeper meaning behind these two commandments is that a father must give to a child in order to let him or her go. As one parenting specialist puts it, we raise our children to leave us.[13]

Teaching to Swim

Some commentators say the commandment for a father to teach his child to swim ought to be taken literally, for one is teaching a child a necessary and perhaps lifesaving skill. In Babylonia, where this teaching originated, there were multiple rivers, so this was certainly a piece of practical advice.

The instruction also can be understood as a metaphor. Teaching children to keep "their heads above water" is really teaching them independence and self-sufficiency. In a way, it summarizes all the preceding commandments. By allowing inevitable pain into your children's lives (as symbolized by circumcision); shielding them so that they can approach challenges when they are ready (redemption); giving them a moral compass, a sense of belonging, and an appreciation of the spiritual (teaching Torah); and respecting their choices in terms of family life and profession (marriage and teaching a trade), you ultimately teach them to swim in life. This gives them both the support and the space they need to enable them to grow into the people they are meant and want to be. Not unlike other close relationships, Jewish law tells us that when it comes to raising a child, you "push with the left hand and caress with the right" (Babylonian Talmud, *Sotah* 47a).

It is also notable what the list does not include. It does not say "love." This may be because the authors of this piece of Talmud felt that the love of a father was so obvious it did not need to be mentioned. Alternatively, it could be because love is a very difficult thing to command. The only two places in the Torah where we are instructed to love is to love the stranger and to love God (Leviticus 19:18, 19:34; Deuteronomy 6:5). But these forms of love are primarily abstract, implying empathy and duty. They are not the flesh-and-blood, messy love that comes with living with another human being. Rather than be commanded, such love must be born out of freedom.

"As a Father Carries a Child"

It is without question that love is a basis for true fatherhood. Another metaphor in Jewish tradition illustrates this idea. When the Israelites came out of Egypt from slavery into the independent world of the wilderness, a biblical poem tells us:

> Like an eagle who rouses his nestlings,
> gliding down to his young,
> so did God spread wings and take them,
> bearing them on pinions. (Deuteronomy 32:11)

In this poem, God is compared to a father eagle who lovingly cares for his young. The eagle bears them on his wings to guide them to the Land of Israel. Elsewhere, the Torah explicitly states that God carried the people "as a man carries his son" (Deuteronomy 1:31). The commentator Rashi beautifully elaborates:

> God directed them [the Israelites] with compassion and sensitivity like the eagle which is compassionate toward his children and does not enter the nest startlingly but rather beats and flaps with his wings above his young, going between tree and tree and branch and branch, so that his children may wake up and be strong enough to receive him.... He does not weigh down upon them but floats over them, touching them yet not touching them. (Rashi on Deuteronomy 32:11)

In the same way one must hold a baby bird, solid enough to support it but not too powerful as to crush it, so is there a balancing act of strength and compassion that goes into parenting. We are "touching them yet not touching them." The human spirit is awakened gradually in children, and it takes patience and self-awareness, closeness and distance, to enable them to grow into self-sufficient adults.

AVINU MALKEINU:
THE COMPASSIONATE SIDE OF THE EQUATION

Too often men find themselves cast into confining stereotypical roles. Just as men have historically been expected to be breadwinners, often men are expected to be the primary disciplinarian to their children. "Just wait until your father gets home" is a frequent refrain in many homes.

"I hate it when she does that," a man we will call Dan says about his wife while sitting in my office. Sometimes, the rabbi's office is the first stop on the way to marital counseling. "I get home from work, and they go running."

"That is not a good feeling," I say, attempting to validate his emotions.

"No, it really isn't. It's really unfair. But the kids listen to me more," he continues. "They don't listen to her the way they listen to me."

In one respect, there is a certain amount of satisfaction for a man knowing his word is law. Dan explains, "There is a certain limit beyond which my kids know they may not push me. I don't know if they have that with their mother. They know that when they are disrespectful or cross a certain line, I mean business. Maybe I'm too harsh."

I responded that the problem doesn't seem to me to be that Dan is too harsh a disciplinarian. The problem appears to be that somehow it has become his job to discipline the children, while his wife gets to take on a softer, kinder role. Perhaps she needs to step up to the tough job of being fair, firm, and following through?

"But what do I do when I come home and they have really done something wrong?"

"How about nothing?" He looks at me curiously. "How about refusing to be defined by that role and instead coaching your wife to help her more effectively discipline the kids? Maybe she needs some sense of empowerment."

While being the punisher appears to be a societal norm for fathers, another side of Jewish tradition challenges this notion of father-as-disciplinarian. It surfaces every year during the Days of Awe, Rosh Hashanah and Yom Kippur.

The central theme of the High Holy Days is the metaphor of God as *Avinu Malkeinu,* translated directly as "our Father, our King." On these days, we sit in judgment of ourselves and our transgressions. We think of God as looking into our hearts and asking us to repent for our misdeeds. As in other places in Jewish tradition, we liken God to a father. But rather than the father who solely judges and punishes, the prayer book invokes just the opposite:

> Our Father, our King, be gracious and answer us, even though we have little merit. Act toward us with generosity, loving-kindness, and save us.... Just as we are Your children, be compassionate to us the way a father is compassionate toward his children.[14]

The image of a father here is a complicated one. On the one hand, the themes of judgment and punishment are still present. We deserve punishment for our transgressions, the liturgy says, but God, as a Father, chooses not to punish us out of a sense of mercy. Does this reduce the emotional breadth of a father's compassion to having pity on those whom he should punish? A deeper look into the liturgy reveals that the image of father symbolizes more than mercy. These song lyrics symbolize nurturing and protective love:

> We are Your people
> You are our King.
> We are Your children
> You are our Father.
> We are Your possession
> You are our Portion.
> We are Your flock
> You are our Shepherd.
> We are Your vineyard
> You are our Keeper.
> We are Your beloved
> You are our Friend.[15]

The images of Father and King are rooted, in the end, in the less power-laden metaphors of Keeper and Friend. The poem claims that as a shepherd looks after sheep, or as a vintner carefully waters and gently cultivates a vineyard, so does God, as a Father, care for us. God does so because we are God's beloved. (The prayer also demonstrates that conceiving of God as a Father or Shepherd is not Christianity's exclusive domain but rather has roots in Judaism and is an area of commonality.) To be a father, the prayer implies, means to be loving and not just silently, but demonstratively. This is a father who nurtures his children.

There is much debate in liberal congregations today about what to make of the *Avinu Malkeinu* prayer. Some find its references to God as Father and King off-putting, invoking a history of patriarchal oppression. On the other hand, the word "father" has far more emotional impact than the word "parent" can ever have. A compromise has been to leave the Hebrew untranslated and let people wrestle with their own sense of meaning.

One of the positive aspects in thinking of God as *Avinu Malkeinu* is that it gives us permission to shed the stereotype of being a disciplinarian and to explore a wider range of emotions. Men, as modeled by God, are entitled to be compassionate, caring and nurturing fathers. In addition to being authoritarian, these ideals, too, are available to us.

Anger and Rebellion: The Defiant Son

Here's a story from Rabbinic literature I learned from the Jewish educator and writer Joel Lurie Grishaver:[16]

Once there was a prince who lived in a palace with his father, the king. The prince became engaged to a lovely girl, and the father was delighted. He made all of the wedding plans, decorated the palace, and spent a fortune. His most extravagant expenditure was a *chuppah*, a wedding canopy, the likes of which had never been seen on earth. It was unbelievably beautiful.

Then, one day, as the wedding approached, the father accidentally walked in on his son having sexual relations with a girl who was not his intended. The king flew into a rage, tearing down the palace's decorations and breaking everything in sight. With zeal the father demolished the *chuppah*, shattering it into pieces.

The people of the kingdom went into mourning. But the prince's tutor, a wise teacher, walked into the wedding hall and did a strange thing. He picked up one of the broken poles of the *chuppah* and carved a flute from it. Once finished, he began to play. The people were shocked.

"At a time like this, when the king is beside himself with fury, how can you play music?"

"I am playing music," the teacher replied, "because when the father lashed out in anger, he struck down the *chuppah* and not his son" (Lamentations Rabbah 4:14).

The Sages told this story for two reasons. First, our children can disappoint us. They behave badly or in incomprehensible ways. We can feel great anger, even rage, at their behavior. Nevertheless, our task, the Sages teach, is to make sure we control our anger appropriately. If we need to hit something, we hit the *chuppah* instead of our child. We should recall: "Who is strong?" "The one who controls his impulses" (*Pirkei Avot* 4:1).

Another reason the Rabbis told this story was that they knew what it was like to disappoint. The Rabbis, in telling this story, created a parable about their historic situation. For them, the king was God, and they were the prince. The wedding canopy represented the Temple in Jerusalem, which was destroyed first by the Babylonians in 586 BCE and then by the Romans in 70 CE. The Rabbis understood the destruction of the Temple to be a punishment for their infidelity in "trooping to the harlot's house" of other gods (Jeremiah 5:7). They felt they had betrayed the covenant of love and responsibility to which they were accountable.

Perhaps the secret of the story is to learn from both the father and the son. On the one hand, children can deeply betray and disappoint us. On the other, we recognize that we are far from perfect ourselves. The key appears to not do anything that permanently ruptures the relationship, as this second story, which completes the first, shows:

The king, deeply grieved by his son's betrayal, banished him from the palace. In his anger, he swore a foolish oath. He swore that the son would never be allowed into the palace again.

After some time, the father and the son wished to be reconciled. But the father had taken a vow, and in fact, the palace as it stood reminded him too much of the past. How could he bring his son back into that place?

"I swore that my son would not enter this palace," the king declared. "Instead, I will tear it down and build a new one, and that is the palace my son and I will share" (Ecclesiastes Rabbah 10:20).

In this concluding parable, another building gets destroyed, but the circumstances are different. Here, the building is cleared away to make room for a new relationship and a new foundation of trust. A trauma can be transformed into a new beginning so long as the relationship is never cut off.

We are entitled to be angry when our children disappoint. But sometimes we have to look very closely at both our anger and our expectations. If our child has transgressed an ethical boundary, then our anger is appropriate and deserved. If our child simply isn't doing what we want, perhaps we have to rethink our expectations.

INEVITABLE DISAPPOINTMENT:
BUT WHO'S TO BLAME?

Psychologist Brad E. Sachs cautions against reacting in an unhealthy way to a child's misbehavior.[17] Perhaps you've blamed your child. Perhaps you've blamed others. Perhaps you've blamed yourself. Perhaps you've distanced yourself from your child or, alternatively, have become overprotective and hyper-involved in your child's life. While all of these "solutions" have benefits, they fail to address the problem and help the child meet life's challenges in a healthy way.

Sometimes a child's problems stem from the unrealistic expectations placed on him or her. Too often, a child's arrival is anticipated with dreams for that child that can never be fulfilled. As men, we think of all of the things our fathers did wrong, and we swear we will never make the same mistakes. We think how much better it will be when, as Sachs puts it, our Perfect Child arrives and we become the Perfect Parent who feels love in ways we have never before felt. Instead, our child soon proves to be imperfect, and so do we. While we are moved to great depths of love, our child screams or bites or pees on the floor out of spite, or sneaks out of the house, or doesn't study and fails at math, or talks back or does any of a host of other infuriating things.

In fact, the Torah tells us of the "wayward and defiant son, who does not heed his father or mother and does not obey them even after they discipline him" (Deuteronomy 21:18). In a violent fantasy, the Torah tells us that parents can lay hold of such a child and publicly stone him! "I wanted to throttle him!" some parents say. A Talmudic commentary on just such a passage tells us the real story: "There never has been a 'wayward and defiant son,' and never will be" (Babylonian Talmud, *Sanhedrin* 71a). Before utterly condemning a child, look inward to determine whether the cause of your disappointment and anger is the child or your own expectations.

Because of this inevitable disappointment, Sachs teaches that with every child there are really three births. The first is when we discover we are going to have a child. In our minds, we create a fantasy. "This is the dream child who will flawlessly meet all of our expectations for perfection and remedy all the defects of the unavoidably flawed parent-child relationship we ourselves had to endure."[18] The second birth shatters our dream when the child arrives into the world, screaming, growing, and later testing all our boundaries. We can be filled with frustration. If we are fortunate enough, however, there can be a third birth of the child as he or she, released from our unrealistic expectations, grows to meet his or her own needs instead of our own.

"I was a premed major for six years," a friend once told me. "Six years of miserable college because my father desperately wanted 'my son, the doctor.' It's like a Jewish obsession! I was not a great student, and I was clueless in biology.

"I finally stood up to him and told him I was switching my major to business. It was either that or flunk out. And after all, if it was good enough for him, why couldn't it be good enough for me? He always said that he wanted better for me than what he had, but being a doctor just simply wasn't it. I liked my dad's kind of work, and I enjoy doing it now.

"The funny thing is, looking back at that time, we would have never known that I would go into the family business. My father and I now work side by side every day. We have never been closer."

We contribute to our own disappointment in a child with inappropriate expectations. Recognizing this, we become better parents by forgiving a child for not obediently fulfilling our impossible hopes and dreams. Sometimes it means tearing down a palace and being willing to build a new one, but the reward is that we create a lifelong relationship of love and renewal.

FATHERING AN ADOPTED CHILD

Additional opportunities for fathering are becoming more wide-spread today. Adoption is one of them. In Jewish families, not only is the frequency of adoption increasing but so is transracial adoption. China, the republics of the former Soviet Union, Korea, and Guatemala are among the nations from which North American Jews are adopting children. The latest National Jewish Population survey finds that over 5 percent of Jewish families include an adopted child, totaling about thirty-five thousand children. That's a considerable increase from previous years.[19]

The result is that today's Jewish family is more likely to include a palate of skin colors and backgrounds, making synagogues and other Jewish institutions more diverse. This diversity is an occasion to be celebrated. Not only have imperiled children found a safe home, but the Jewish people are strengthened as our sense of connectedness to other peoples is heightened.

Nevertheless, "nonwhite" adopted children are a minority within a minority, which can cause them tremendous anxiety. For this reason, the Jewish Multiracial Network was formed "to build a community of Jews of color and multiracial Jewish families for mutual support, learning, and empowerment."[20]

In addition to the host of questions any parent faces raising an adopted child, Jewish fathers face some very specific ones related to Jewish tradition:

- Do Jewish sources differentiate between adopted and biological children?
- What are my rights as the father of an adopted child? What are my duties?
- If the child is a boy, do I need to circumcise him?
- What Hebrew name do I give an adopted child?
- Can I name my child after my relatives, or do I need to honor the birth family?
- As Hebrew names include one's parents' names (*ben*—son of/*bat*—daughter of), which name do I use to indicate lineage?

- Is a converted child *ben/bat Avraham v'Sarah,* that is, a "child of Abraham and Sarah" as with other converts, or named with my Hebrew name?
- Does this child need to honor me in the same way any other child needs to "honor your father and mother"?

Who Is Called Father?

The answer to many of these questions may be summarized by this Rabbinic statement: "He who raises a child is called 'Father,' not the one who gives him life" (Exodus Rabbah 46:5). Judaism has long praised the adoption of orphans. The Torah claims that God "upholds the cause of the fatherless" (Deuteronomy 10:18), and therefore we should follow suit. The prophet Isaiah tells us:

> Learn to do good.
> Devote yourselves to justice;
> Aid the wronged.
> Uphold the rights of the orphan. (Isaiah 1:17)

We also find several biblical examples of people adopting children and raising them as their own, most prominently Mordecai raising his cousin Esther. The Hebrew Bible says that Mordecai "was foster father to Hadassah—that is, Esther—his uncle's daughter, for she had neither father nor mother.... Mordecai adopted her as his own daughter" (Esther 2:7). This adopted child goes on to be one of the greatest heroines of Jewish history and the key player celebrated on the holiday of Purim.

It is not just in biblical times that we see adoption affirmed. The Talmud also echoes: "Whoever brings up an orphan in his home is as if he gave birth to the child" (Babylonian Talmud, *Sanhedrin* 19b). This teaches that when one adopts a child, one inherits all obligations of a biological parent. Historically, a Jewish court had the power to create this relationship, as the court was considered in Jewish law to be the ultimate "father of orphans" that acted on behalf of defenseless children (Babylonian Talmud, *Gittin* 37a).

Contemporary Jewish authorities have clarified that a child's racial or ethnic background ought to have absolutely no impact on the raising of a child. The same obligations described in the Talmud pertain to all Jewish children. The community is likewise obligated to embrace each child as fully Jewish and created in the divine image, just as with any convert to Judaism. Unfortunately, the reality is that the Jewish community is just as subject to the ugliness of prejudice and bigotry as any other. This is an evil that must be consciously opposed. Instead of the harmful focus on skin color, we can celebrate the diversity of heritage that has always been a part of the Jewish people. Jews have never been all "white." Jews have long been a global people, with darker skin in Mediterranean countries, the Middle East, India, and Ethiopia, and with Asian features among the Jews of China, for example. Jews do not come in one color.

Adoptive Jewish parents should celebrate the racial and cultural heritage of a child's birth country even as they bring that into the Jewish fold. Naming ceremonies and rites of *b'nei mitzvah* are opportunities to affirm a child's identity. In the words of adoptive father Yosef Abramowitz, we not only must affirm that we are all made *b'tzelem Elohim*, in God's image, but also must reinterpret *tzelem Yehudi*, the image of the Jew, and reexamine *tzelem kehilah*, the image of our community.[21] Ultimately, this is a question of how loving we truly are.

In terms of Jewish ritual, we must proceed sensitively. Jewish law teaches that we should circumcise adopted boys, as in any conversion process. This, of course, depends upon the child's health, but the earlier the better. We must take into account a child's age and let compassion be our guide.

Naming, however, follows a different procedure. The Hebrew name given an adopted child may honor the adoptive parents' family. Similarly, the majority of Jewish legal authorities hold that the child's Hebrew name follows the adoptive parents, so that rather than being *ben/bat Avraham v'Sarah* like a convert to Judaism, the child is named *ben/bat* with the Hebrew names of the adoptive parents following. This ruling has been legitimated by all denominations of Judaism.[22]

In addition, adopted children need to honor their adoptive parents. When an adoptive parent dies, the adopted child should say *Kaddish*, the traditional Jewish prayer of mourning, for him or her. An adoptive father is a parent of the adopted child in every respect. While some children may later seek out their biological parents, this in no way changes the relationship owed to the adoptive parents from the point of view of Jewish tradition.

Judaism has long considered adoption a *mitzvah*, a sacred obligation incorporating the commandments to "be fertile and increase" (Genesis 1:28) with being an advocate for children in need of parents. Adoption is not just accepted; it is to be encouraged. The father of an adopted child is not only a full parent but also an advocate for justice. Taking into account the aging and shrinking of the Jewish population in the Western hemisphere, as well as the trauma faced by many infertile couples, adoption should be thought of as a gift from God. We are very blessed to see our community growing in this way today. To be a father of an adopted child is a special privilege.

FATHERING A STEPCHILD

The number of Jewish stepfathers also is greater than ever, as Jews, along with virtually every other group in contemporary society, experience unprecedented rates of divorce and remarriage.[23] Like adoption, this modern phenomenon has ancient precedents in Jewish law and life. Unlike adoption, the special challenge of being a stepfather is that such a man often takes on the parental duties while receiving few of the rights.

A distinction needs to be made between Western, democratic thinking versus a traditional Jewish perspective. In Western culture and family law, lawsuits resulting from child custody and visitation rights disputes are proliferating. Judaism, however, is a religion of commandments. Even in the most liberal interpretations, Judaism speaks of the dictates of conscience as given by God, not freedoms. Rather than our rights, it principally concerns itself with our obligations. We do not find much discussion in Jewish literature on the rights a man has over a child, but rather the duties to which we are bound. This is extremely important in cases of divorce and remarriage. Whether or not a man has custody over his children or the right to visit them does not impact his obligations toward his children.

In Jewish law, there is the precedent of the *apotropos*, or "guardian." The word comes from Greek, and it is used by the Sages whenever a Jewish man is the custodian over another's dependents or property.[24] The presumption of Jewish law is that the guardian is present to do what is best for the ward. For instance, it says in the Mishnah that when a man supports minors who are not his children, he can freely take money from funds set aside for their welfare to pay their financial obligations. The guardian takes an oath that he only does so in the child's best interest (*Mishnah Gittin* 4:7; Babylonian Talmud, *Gittin* 52a).

Thus there is the balancing act of recognizing the obligations of a natural father and the realm of guardianship of a stepfather. If the natural father is deceased, completely absent, or determined by the court to be a harmful influence, the stepfather's realm of influence increases. If the biological father is present in a child's life, the stepfather's domain is diminished. In all cases, it is the Sages' hope that the guardian is faithful and trustworthy according to the Torah (Babylonian Talmud, *Bava Metzia* 70a). He is present, in an almost completely selfless manner, to protect and guide a child's growth.

In addition to the legal ramifications of a stepfather's role, the Torah also addresses a stepfather's emotions. A stepfather can be an emotional caregiver, not just a material provider. The principle that "he who raises a child is called 'Father'" can apply here as well. In fact, Moses is called the father of the children of his brother

Aaron, even though Aaron was alive and present in their life. The Rabbis explain that any man who is a guide and teacher has the possibility of being a kind of father. A stepfather can be a "Moses" to a child (Babylonian Talmud, *Sanhedrin* 19b).

Similarly, stepfathers can take part in the life-cycle rituals of a child's upbringing. One authority explicitly states that a stepfather ought to be called to the Torah for a child's bar/bat mitzvah, so long as the honor is conveyed with sensitivity and depending upon the officiating rabbi's best judgment.[25] Such honors at other ceremonies, including circumcision and weddings, are likewise beautiful ways to honor a stepfather.

Family life can be volatile, and a stepparent enters the situation with certain disadvantages. A stepparent can never replace a biological parent—love is almost always unfair and unequal—and there is a constant tension between being firm and not overstepping boundaries. But the opportunity remains to create joy, to be a positive influence in a child's life, and to view the opportunity to raise any child as a gift from God.[26]

"Love Him More"

Perhaps a Chasidic story about Rabbi Yisrael ben Eliezer, known as the Baal Shem Tov or the "Besht" and the founder of Chasidic Judaism, best summarizes a father's deepest duty. The story illustrates what any parent eventually goes through as they face their child's growth and inevitable rebellion. It is all the more poignant for men who strive hard to live up to the traditional role of being the authority in a home. To put this story in a contemporary light, allow me to retell it in modern language:

Once there was a Jewish man who had a teenage son. His son, who was so sweet when he was little, was a changed being as an adolescent. His son tested him at every turn. Every conversation seemed to turn into an argument. Every request was challenged. Grounding him and taking away his privileges had no effect. Yelling at him just led to more yelling. The man felt terrible, for it seemed like all he did was yell. He was getting very tired.

In desperation, he went to see his rabbi. This embarrassed the man, who felt more than a little ashamed that he had allowed his religious observance to wane. Would the rabbi judge him harshly? Perhaps the rabbi would feel that the man's problems stemmed from his lapsed observance. The rabbi, however, did not seem to judge him. He greeted him gently as he motioned to a chair.

The man explained his problem to the rabbi. He spoke of how exhausted he was by his relationship with his son. Nothing he did seemed to change his son's behavior. His son seemed determined to avoid all responsibility. The foul language, the disrespect, and the son's constant lying about his whereabouts drove him mad. What could he do to bring his son back to the life he wanted for him?

The rabbi said, "Love him more."

"Of course I love him. But what more am I supposed to do?" asked the exasperated man.

"You must love him more. God loves us despite what we human beings deserve. God sustains us, provides for us, and gives to us, even though we may behave abominably. Just as God loves us, so must you love your son. Eventually, your son will be out of your house, and he will be responsible for his own choices. You will not be able to live his life for him. You will give him the freedom of will that God gave to us. But you can tell him, all the more, how much you love him. Your son will always remember, no matter how far he strays, that you love him. Love him even more for the struggles that he endures. It is all you can do."[27]

READING TORAH ON BEHALF OF A CHILD WHO CAN'T

David and Laura are the parents of four boys. They describe three of their boys as "typical." They are full of energy and can be found running around the sanctuary of the synagogue. When

I enter, the boys assure me that all of the microphones work (they have tested them by screaming into them) and that the cantor's guitar (which they have also tested) sounds good. I say a quick prayer as I whisper to our cantor that he better make sure his guitar is still in one piece.

However, David and Laura's firstborn, Alec, is severely disabled, with the mental capacity of an infant. He is wheelchair-bound and needs constant care and attention. While his younger brothers excel in theater and soccer, Alec will forever remain who he is today.

When Alec was born he suffered a brain trauma that the doctors were uncertain he would survive. David went so far as to call a funeral home and alert the rabbi that he would soon need his services. But days turned into weeks, which turned into months, which turned into years. Alec had other plans.

David and Laura shed many tears for the child Alec was and for the child he might have been. Endless decisions had to be made about Alec's care and residence. They bravely went on to have three more children. Alec cannot converse or communicate in conventional ways, but he can laugh. Sometimes he laughs for no apparent reason; his family finds his laughter contagious.

As the boys grew, David wondered what he should do when Alec turned thirteen. Nothing, he supposed. After all, technically Alec would never achieve the status of bar mitzvah, a religiously responsible adult. Alec will forever remain a child. Jewish law considers Alec a *shoteh*, a person of such diminished intellect that they are not responsible for keeping God's commandments.

Still, the feeling kept nagging at David that attention must be paid in some way to Alec's coming of age. It was when their second-born, anxious to get to his bar mitzvah ceremony, offered to read Torah on behalf of Alec that David realized what he must do. It was not the duty of a younger child to stand in for Alec; his bar mitzvah would come in time. It was a father's duty.

We scheduled an appointment, and David started studying Torah. He confessed to being a much more eager student this time around than when he was an adolescent. When they picked a date for Alec's blessing, they chose according to the weekly Torah portion that would be most meaningful for them. The date and portion that David and Laura picked came from Genesis, in which Abraham and Sarah's son, Isaac, is born. Their choice revolved around the phrase that "Sarah laughed" (Genesis 18:12) at Isaac's birth. This, they felt, captured Alec's laugh and the laughter that he has brought to them.

Similarly, the Haftarah portion for that week (the supplemental portion from the biblical section Prophets), 2 Kings 4:1–37, speaks of a son's birth followed by his near-death experience. In this story, also read during the Shabbat service, the boy is brought back to life and given back to his mother. Again, David and Laura felt this portion most appropriate for Alec's situation. They understood that the sorrows and joys we experience today are not all that different from what people experienced in the past. The Torah's story was their story.

The day came, and David chanted Torah beautifully on behalf of his son. Alec was in his wheelchair in the front row, surrounded by family. Grandparents, aunts, uncles, and other family and friends were all present to celebrate, as was much of the congregation in a heartfelt display of love and support. After reading from the Torah and sharing the Haftarah portion, David and Laura shared Alec's story.

With his parents' prayers still resonating, we wheeled Alec in front of the ark, underneath the *ner tamid* (the "eternal light" representing God's constant presence). There we blessed him. Tears flowed freely. Alec's brothers watched, taking it all in. They also participated in the service, reading prayers. They will remember their brother's bar mitzvah just as much as they will remember their own.

David felt overwhelmed by the response from his family and the community. "It was great to have our extended family together for an occasion that was specific to Alec. The last time that happened, it was during the traumatic events surrounding his birth, when Alec was near death. This was a much different occasion, a positive and uplifting event that celebrated his life. I had always wanted the opportunity to speak about Alec, and our experiences as his parents, to our friends and family. I hope that the service helped Alec's brothers to understand that Alec is a very important part of our family and that the service reflected his importance.

"As a Jewish experience, preparing for and participating in the service was very special for me. Learning my Torah portion was interesting, challenging, and hugely rewarding. I loved learning the Hebrew and the *trope* [the chanting for the Torah portion]. I'll never forget carrying the Torah around the sanctuary, and seeing the joy in people's faces as they leaned over to touch their *siddurim* [prayer books] against it."

For those of us who are blessed with healthy children, it should be humbling to remember just how blessed we really are. We should also keep in mind the extraordinary lengths to which some must go in order to be parents and to pass down the Torah's wisdom to the next generation. Not only Alec was blessed that day. So were his brothers, his father and mother, and all who were gathered as witnesses. When David read Torah on behalf of his child, he taught all of us.

What I Screamed at 3:00 a.m.

My most disappointing moment as a father occurred not with my child but with myself. Far more crushing than realizing I do not have the Perfect Child is realizing I am not the Perfect Parent and that I do not always meet the standards that Jewish tradition lays out for me.

It was approximately three in the morning. My child was crying. The crying had gone on for several hours. Every time we went into the room, the screaming would stop, and the minute we left, it would start again. This went on for several nights in a row.

I was extremely sleep deprived. After listening to the screams for hours, my anxiety built to a breaking point. It was not supposed to be this way! I marched into the room, held that little face in my hands, and screamed: "YOU MUST GO TO SLEEP! YOU MUST! THIS IS VERY BAD, BAD BEHAVIOR! GOOD CHILDREN SLEEP AT NIGHT, DON'T YOU UNDERSTAND! AAAAAAHHHHH!"

This, of course, did not calm my child. To make matters worse, when my wife told me that my stomping about and screaming upset her, I responded by blaming her, arguing that I had to work in the morning and needed more than four hours sleep in five days to function properly.

It was not my best moment. As my heart rate eventually slowed down, I was filled with a deep shame. I felt like the worst father and husband in the world, unworthy of being anywhere near my family. I went back into the room to make sure my fingers hadn't inadvertently bruised my child's face. They hadn't. That far I had not gone.

The next day, a rabbi friend of mine happened to stop into my office. He noticed the bags under my eyes. I was grateful to be able to talk about what happened the night before. "Now you know," he said, "that you are just like the rest of us."

The Hebrew Bible tells us about a similar realization by the prophet Elijah. Elijah hopes to succeed where others had failed. He dedicates his life's work to improving the world. He points out faults and corruption and how things could be better. But he finds that his message falls on deaf ears, and he is forced to flee for his life. His work seems to come to nothing. He runs to the wilderness, heartbroken, and collapses to the ground. Distraught, he prays, "Now, Eternal One, take my life, for I am no better than my fathers" (1 Kings 19:3–4).[28]

Elijah wants to die when he realizes he has failed, that he is nothing special. In fact, he was no more successful than were his fathers. Elijah had sworn he would do better than his fathers did, that he would somehow exceed them. He would be stronger, kinder, and greater. Collapsing in the dirt, he melodramatically thinks his efforts in life are done. It is a moment of utter despair.

While Elijah clearly meant his historical forefathers, the feelings also apply to actual fatherhood. We also experience this despair when we fall short of the expectations we set for ourselves as fathers, as parents.

Perhaps the most necessary ingredient for a man to become a father is forgiveness. We need to forgive our parents for either being too wonderful or too negligent. In finding that forgiveness, we can also find forgiveness for ourselves when we disappoint. In turn, we may be more compassionate and forgiving to our children.

We cannot be perfect. We will fail. Even God, when creating the world, only achieved "very good" (Genesis 1:31) but not "perfect."[29] We, made of imperfect matter, strive for ideals, but we inevitably do not reach them.

Nevertheless, we must always strive. Seek to improve and be better. Remember that we are only human. "The spirituality of imperfection begins with the recognition that trying to be perfect is the most tragic human mistake."[30]

It is a mitzvah *to be a compassionate father, stepfather, or mentor toward children, to not be defined only by being a disciplinarian but to be a man strong enough to demonstrate love. We are additionally commanded to be a role model of Torah in word and deed and, whenever possible, to personally teach Torah to our children. But it is also a* mitzvah *to forgive others and ourselves, living up to God's expectations of "very good" and not "perfect."*

The wonderful thing about not being perfect is that we always have space to improve.

Questions for Reflection

- What hopes or expectations do or did you have for fatherhood? If you are a father, what surprises were there?
- What do you think a man owes a child as his fatherly duty? What do you think of the list of obligations in the Talmud?

- Do you believe men are expected to be the primary disciplinarians in a family?

- Jewish tradition holds that whoever raises or teaches a child is like a father. Have you been a "father" in this way to a child?

- What is your greatest disappointment as a father? How have you dealt with it?

6

A Man within a Sacred Community

It is no secret that a serious gender gap is negatively impacting liberal synagogues and some other Jewish institutions. Women generally outnumber men two to one at synagogue events. A recent survey of Reform congregations conducted by Doug Barden found:

> There is mounting statistical evidence, that at any given national NFTY youth [North American Federation of Temple Youth] event, for example, there will be a ratio of 65% girls to 35% boys.... A review of HUC-JIR [Hebrew Union College—Jewish Institute of Religion, the Reform rabbinic seminary] enrollment figures indicates the ratio of female to male first year rabbinic HUC-JIR students is now approaching a 70%/30% ratio.... The figure of 80% female, 20% male is often quoted when it comes to the expected attendees at a local temple adult education program.[1]

Liberal synagogues are not alone in facing a gender gap. Churches confront this phenomenon as well. David Murrow, in his book *Why Men Hate Going to Church*, reports, "The typical American church-goer is a woman.... There are more women (61%) than men

(39%) in the pews.... Today 20 to 25 percent of America's married, churchgoing women regularly attend without their husbands."[2] In a statistical survey of churches in America, he finds that most churches report at least a 12 percent gender gap, with Presbyterian/Reformed and Episcopal churches having the largest imbalance.[3] Murrow describes a scene in church that could well apply to many synagogues:

> I studied the bulletin: all of the midweek and volunteer opportunities were pitched at women and children. Each announcement ended with a woman's name: "For more information call Shari/Sarah/Andrea/Victoria/Lauren, etc." I looked around at the men. Most were present in body only. Truth be told, the only man in the room who was truly engaged was the pastor, who, as he clicked past the twenty-five minute mark in his sermon, seemed to be picking up steam, even as the men in the crowd were losing theirs.[4]

Why is "male flight" becoming so prevalent?[5] I believe the main reasons for this gender gap are a change of priorities among men and the loss of leisure time. As I've documented elsewhere in this book, men today work longer hours and drive lengthier commutes. Consequently, they would rather spend their reduced free time with family and attending events for their children. Men are now partners in household responsibilities and raising the kids, and time just does not seem to allow for Friday night or Saturday morning services. In addition, more and more women have found the synagogue enlivening, and they have shared it with their friends. When a task needs doing, women are more likely to ask other women to pitch in. With women leading services and committees, too often the liberal synagogue broadcasts the message that men are not really needed.[6]

Another reason why some men forgo synagogue attendance is that too often the synagogue simply fails them. Sometimes the failures are small. Other times they are significant.

Some common complaints include:

- The synagogue's sound system seems to be run by amateurs.
- The website is hopelessly out of date.
- The office cannot seem to spell my name correctly.
- The Hebrew is baffling, and I'm embarrassed by my ignorance.
- The cantor wants me to sing, God forbid, out loud.
- The sermon drags on, and I find myself dozing off; how can I be expected to listen to an entire sermon when I can't sit through a television show without changing channels every few seconds?
- And finally, all the synagogue ever seems to do is ask me for money; dues keep increasing even though I hardly attend. Is it really worth it?

Before dismissing the synagogue as irrelevant, boring, and amateurish, however, ask yourself, with all humility, whether you're being unjustifiably cynical. If you believe Judaism has been a valuable civilization and deserves a future, then its central institution, the synagogue, needs men's talents more than unconstructive criticism. Rather than looking for the worst in the synagogue, look at the same phenomena as opportunities where you can be of help. It is, in fact, precisely men's expertise that the synagogue needs. Look at the synagogue's shortcomings not as excuses to walk away but as challenges you can address.

A change in how you conceptualize the synagogue may be in order. Instead of thinking of yourself as merely a consumer of the synagogue's products (High Holy Day tickets, religious school for our kids, a hall for the bar/bat mitzvah party), think of yourself as a member of a community. Rather than paying dues and fees, view the transaction as contributing to the community's benefit—and hence your own, since you and your family are a part of the very same community. Rather than asking whether you are getting enough bang for your buck, ask yourself how you can contribute to the greater good.

This shift in thinking is difficult, in men especially, because modern life conditions us to put individual needs ahead of communal responsibilities. It is not just a gender gap the synagogue faces. It is a cultural chasm.

The Bill of Rights versus the Torah

When I ask parents what they pray for at the time of their child's bar/bat mitzvah, after health and happiness I inevitably hear comments like these:

"I want him to be able to stand on his own two feet."

"I hope this process has increased her self-esteem."

"I want him to know that if he puts his mind to it, he can accomplish anything."

"I wish that she always knows that we are there for her and love her."

There tend to be slight variations in the prayers for boys versus girls. For girls, the prayers for self-esteem and that she should always know that she is loved place her squarely in the context of family. It's different for boys. Parents often mention the importance of family to their boys. But the focus is invariably on independence and accomplishment, which while important in our society can also be interpreted as conflicting with communal needs. We want our children, and especially our boys, to be able to "make it on their own."

This emphasis on the self is central to Western culture and, perhaps even more so, to the idealized American way, which has been propagated all over the world. Globalized American values include rugged individualism, to be able to survive in a competitive world through aggressive self-reliance. The family is there to be supportive, but many of us seem most proud when boys break out on their own and show independence.

Consider the epitome of this outlook, the Declaration of Independence of the United States. We read about "life, liberty, and the pursuit of happiness." We sing about "the land of the free and the home of the brave." Patrick Henry declared, "Give me liberty or give me death!" American philosopher Ralph Waldo Emerson wrote an entire tract entitled "Self-Reliance."

Western democratic culture has enshrined as a holy value the freedom of the individual, where each individual can vote his or her own conscience and act in any way that does not infringe upon the rights of others. The central document in the United States that embodies this idea is the Bill of Rights, which constitutes the first ten amendments to the U.S. Constitution. They include freedom of speech, freedom of the press, and freedom of religion.

Compare the Bill of Rights with its tone and emphasis to another set of ten, the Ten Commandments. Both share the qualities of being laws concerned with human welfare, but the similarities stop there. Rather than speaking the language of freedom of the individual and the rights of each person, the Ten Commandments address our obligations to those outside of ourselves. Honor your father and mother; keep Shabbat; do not murder, commit adultery, or steal. The Ten Commandments, in fact, hold the individual sacred, but the language is about relationships between people. This sacred text ultimately speaks the language of the collective and the limits of our freedom. Rather than speak to the culture of rights, the Decalogue addresses the commandments we are to follow as a group.

This theme in the Ten Commandments is present throughout the entire Torah. When Moses says, "You shall be holy" (Leviticus 19:1), the Hebrew "you shall" is in the plural. Holiness is a collective aspiration. It is something a community must accomplish together. When Moses gives his final address before dying, he makes sure all strata of the community are present, from the powerful and rich to the vulnerable and those working menial jobs. He looks out over the crowd, and he speaks to the assemblage as a whole, including "your tribal heads, your elders, and your officials, all the men of Israel, your children, your wives, even the stranger within your camp, from woodchopper to water drawer" (Deuteronomy 29:9–11). They are a community, a single unit.

On the whole, American life speaks the language of the individual self while Jewish culture speaks the language of community. The mythological American man is the go-getter who "pulls himself up by his own bootstraps" and achieves self-realization. He is the "self-made man." The Jewish man, on the other hand, is a member of a group. His Hebrew name puts him in the context of family and tribe: *Reuven ben* / son of *Chaim Halevi* / the Levite. In coming to America, many Jewish men joined fraternities—*Landsmanschaft*—structured to reflect the village or region from which they emigrated. They created dense ethnic communities where one's neighborhood was one's group and identity. They grew up in shared bedrooms and houses that held multiple generations.

The pursuit of the American dream has brought us suburban houses with lawns delineated by fences, each individual house standing on its own, or apartment buildings where people meet at the mailbox or in the elevator, seldom sharing a word. Many times neighbors do not know each other.

This is the social environment in which American Jews, in particular, have become more and more dispersed. In an echo of the American pioneering spirit, each Jewish man set out with his family on his own to find his own piece of territory. As a result, Jewish men have ceased to think in terms of community and learned to think in terms of self.

Speaking in terms of community today can be difficult. It often falls on deaf ears. If all you have ever known has been your nuclear family, it's hard to have a communal frame of reference. We believe each person is entitled to their own, private space that should not be violated. And yet, I believe self-fulfillment is only possible in the context of belonging, not isolation.

Imagine what would happen if parents had in mind the importance of community when they offered their prayers for their child on the child's bar/bat mitzvah day. Perhaps they might pray:

"I hope you become an upstanding member of your community."

"I wish for you to learn to always give *tzedakah* [righteous giving] and contribute to the greater good."

"I pray that you see yourself as part of a larger whole and that this leads you to a passion for *tikkun olam* [the repair of the world]."

"You should not just seek blessings for yourself but try to be a blessing to others."

We Invented Social Responsibility: *Tzedakah* and *Gemilut Chasadim*

Jewish men were the ones to set down the Torah's words. Jewish men, mostly rabbis, were also the authors of the discussions that followed in the Talmud and in the different Jewish codes of law. These documents were written by men and meant for other Jewish men to read. They came from a premodern, patriarchal society. Both the credit and the blame belong with Jewish men.

A major theme of this literature is the notion of social responsibility. The idea that we are responsible for each other and not just ourselves, and that we need to give our time and money for the betterment of the whole, is a quintessentially Jewish belief. The Talmud tells us: *Kol Yisrael areivim zeh bazeh*—"Each of the people Israel is responsible one for the other" (Babylonian Talmud, *Shavuot* 39a). We exist not as islands but as a corporate entity that is interdependent. God judges us not just as individuals but as a people, and beyond us, the human race as a whole.

Consider this in light of our social responsibility toward the poor. As early as the time of the Torah in the second and first centuries BCE, the Israelites took on the obligation of helping the needy members of our community, to leaving no one behind. The male Israelite farmer was obligated to protect society's most vulnerable members: the women, orphans, and strangers. Produce from the edges of one's field was purposefully left behind to be gleaned by the poor. Forgotten sheaves and malformed and fallen fruit were similarly left. The Torah repeatedly tells us to think of the poor. Israelite men working the land believed that if they did, not only would they do what was right in God's eyes, but their endeavors would be rewarded. To give was to be blessed (Deuteronomy 24:19–21).

The direct giving of our produce was a commandment from God and an exercise in compassion. The very names the Sages gave for these kinds of produce—the marginal, the left behind, the forgotten, the malformed, and the fallen—sensitized us to the kinds of people who tended to be poor. We were confronted daily by the community's poor and were told not to "hide ourselves" from one in need (Deuteronomy 22:4).

What formerly was the responsibility of each Israelite farmer became the duty of communal institutions. As Jews moved into urban areas, they created community organizations to ensure that the poor and vulnerable would still be aided. In place of agricultural produce, the Jewish people invented the *kupah*, a weekly collection and distribution of money for the poor on Friday before Shabbat. This practice of social responsibility was so common that the philosopher Moses Maimonides wrote, "Never have we seen or heard of a Jewish community that does not have a *kupah*" (*Mishneh Torah, Matnot Aniyyim* 9:3). In addition, some larger communities organized a *tamchui*, a daily distribution of food. All forms of giving were offered to Jews and gentiles alike (*Mishneh Torah, Matnot Aniyyim* 7:7, based on *Mishnah Gittin* 5:8).

This kind of giving, involving either money or some other material substance, is widely known as *tzedakah* (righteous giving). But there is another kind of giving, involving the giving of time, that is seen as even more praiseworthy. Acts of kindness, *gemilut chasadim*, involves not just giving money but also spending time with someone, such as visiting the sick. It involves not just making a donation but also being available to console mourners. *Gemilut chasadim* are gifts of the essence that is at the heart of what we might today call volunteerism.

Our Sages taught: *Gemilut chasadim* are greater than *tzedakah* in three ways. *Tzedakah* is done with one's money, while *gemilut chasadim* are done with one's person or money. *Tzedakah* is given to the poor, while *gemilut chasadim* is given to poor and rich. *Tzedakah* can only be given to the living, while *gemilut chasadim* can be given to the living and the dead (Babylonian Talmud, *Sukkah* 49b).

It is not that *tzedakah* is inadequate. It is that *gemilut chasadim* is simply more generous. Anyone can do acts of kindness, and they can be received by the poor and the rich as well as the living and the dead. According to Jewish law, we are socially responsible for each other's emotional as well as physical well-being.

And yet, the Talmud observes that men seem more prone to give *tzedakah*, while women make themselves more available for *gemilut chasadim*. A parable tells us how the people of a certain village appeal to a Sage named Abba Hilkiah and his wife. The village has been suffering from drought, and the people feel that rain might come if this righteous couple prays on their behalf. In response, both the Sage and his wife stand before God in prayer. They pray for rain together, standing on the roof of their house and beseeching God on behalf of the people. Miraculously, God answers their prayer by sending rain clouds. However, something mysterious happens. The clouds first come to Abba Hilkiah's wife, hovering over her head, and then only afterward do they extend to him. The people of the village watch in awe. Amidst the amazing raindrops, they ask Abba Hilkiah why his wife seemed to merit God's blessing more than he did, as the rain clouds seemed to indicate. He answers, "Because she bakes bread and gives it to the hungry, while I give money" (Babylonian Talmud, *Ta'anit* 23a–23b).

Abba Hilkiah's wife is the more righteous person whose prayers are answered first. Abba Hilkiah's generosity is blessed by God, but the sacrifice of time and personal involvement in giving is even more praiseworthy and receives God's immediate approval. Additionally, Abba Hilkiah's wife likely performed other acts of kindness—a gentle word, an encouraging smile—as she compassionately helped those in need. Writing a check is good, but giving of one's time and energy is even better.

The Gift of Time Is a Gift of Oneself

The Jewish people invented a powerful and all-embracing form of social responsibility. Jewish men codified it into existence. We thought of each member of the community and our obligations to the whole. And while Jewish men have remained generous when it has come to *tzedakah*, the rate of volunteerism among men for acts of kindness is significantly lower than among women.

In a study entitled "Volunteering in America," 32.4 percent of women compared to 25 percent of men were reported to volunteer in some way outside of their careers.[7] As reported in 2006, David Eisner, CEO of the Corporation for National and Community Service, observed, "From schools and shelters to hospitals and hotlines, volunteers are vital to America's social and economic well-being."[8]

All the more so for the Jewish community's well-being. Synagogues, elder care, mentoring programs, charities—almost every Jewish institution depends on *tzedakah* and *gemilut chasadim*. And yet, as noted by Steven M. Cohen and Rabbi Jack Wertheimer in "Whatever Happened to the Jewish People?" the ascent of individualism has resulted in a "waning sense of communal responsibility."[9] Whether it is showing up for a rally on behalf of a Jewish cause or giving to Jewish institutions, both monetary donations and volunteering have declined in recent years.

Cohen and Wertheimer assert that, in North America at least, Judaism has become a private matter of personal spirituality as opposed to a force for social justice. It has become more about quiet meditation than the creation of compassionate communities. This runs counter to hundreds of years of Jewish men giving of themselves in the name of their religion for the betterment of others. Being a responsible Jewish man does not just mean being there for your family. It also means being there for your community—both its Jewish and non-Jewish components.

The gift of time is the gift of oneself. Why is it that women volunteer in much larger numbers than men? Is it a simple function of biology? Are women more generous as a byproduct of their role as nurturing mothers? Is it because women have the time? (I think not; research shows working women volunteer more than working men.)[10] Is it something else? Perhaps it's because men are oriented toward problem solving and find long-term commitments simply unsatisfying?

Frankly, I'm unsure of the answer. But I do know that men who give their time as well as their money to the community find tremendous meaning and satisfaction. Giving of oneself is a spiritual gift with a long history in Judaism. Its cornerstone role for the Jewish future is unquestionable.

What many men do not realize is that giving to the community is also nourishing to the self. Giving time and money for the betterment of the Jewish people and the world at large is not a matter of self-sacrifice. It is a matter of self-fulfillment. The Sage Hillel articulated this truth in his classic three-part question: "If I am not for myself, who will be for me? If I am only for myself, then what am I? If not now, when?" (*Pirkei Avot* 1:14). It is only by balancing duty to ourselves with duty to others that we are all we can be. There is a pressing need for us to do what we can and to understand that the time to do so is now. We can break through our complacency and become a part of something greater.

GIVING THAT ENLIVENS

Volunteerism among men may be down, but it has not disappeared. A friend of mine named Jon is an example.

Jon is a very busy man. He is always on the go; you wonder how he manages. In addition to being an attorney and running his own business, he has a wife and four children. Not only that, he proudly describes himself as a "semi-professional Jewish volunteer."

Jon helps raise money for Combined Jewish Philanthropies of Boston, the name of the local Jewish Federation. This organization raises money that helps fund Jewish camps, education programs in conjunction with synagogues, trips to Israel, nursing homes, and innumerable other projects that are the best part of Jewish people-hood. Jon sees himself as part of a community. When asked why he does what he does, he says simply, "I get a great sense of personal satisfaction from my efforts as a volunteer. I feel that I am making a difference in the lives of others and that I am setting a good example for my children and others."

It is not only personal satisfaction that Jon receives. Being a part of the Jewish community has given him like-minded friends. He also says, "The people I've met through my volunteer efforts have become dear friends and have enriched my life. I feel that I am part of a special community with a common bond forged through a commitment to bettering our world."

Jon gives both in terms of *tzedakah* and *gemilut chasadim*. Both give him great satisfaction. He did not happen to become the kind of Jew he is by accident. "My parents have always been volunteer leaders in their community, even when my siblings and I were young children. They supported Jewish organizations, but also worked with other nonprofits, including arts organizations and health services. They always told us that we had an ethical obliga-tion as Jews and as citizens to give back to our communities with our time and with our resources."

As I said, Jon's a busy guy, yet he always seems to have time to take on more. Moreover, his energy never seems to lag. The rea-son for this is that the joy he receives from volunteering spurs him to take on more. Volunteering energizes Jon. When speaking to other volunteers, he tells them, "Find something that you're pas-sionate about and focus your volunteer efforts on that passion. There are so many ways to help make our world better—don't do something because you're being asked to do it; do it because it gives you joy. Don't be afraid to say 'no' but don't wait to be asked before you say 'yes.'"

"My Cup Runs Over"

The Jewish philosopher Moses Maimonides—also known as the Rambam, from the Hebrew acronym of his title and name—talked about this enlivening aspect of giving of oneself. Maimonides himself was tremendously productive in his life. In addition to being a rabbi and authoring many volumes of Jewish philosophy and law, he served as personal physician to the sultan of Egypt. Still, he felt obligated to also meet with members of his community, serving as their doctor as well. As a pious man, he felt such giving back was commanded of him by God. He kept an exhausting schedule, meeting with the members of his community in the afternoon after getting an early-morning start in fulfilling his other duties. He also found time to teach students and answer letters sent to him from many countries.[11]

Maimonides may have felt commanded by God to give to his community, but he shunned the thought that one should do so in hope of a heavenly reward. Rather, Maimonides taught that one performs the *mitzvah* in hope of drawing close to the Creator, nothing more. By drawing close to God, Maimonides meant that we raise ourselves up through righteous actions above our animal-based instincts and appetites. In short, Maimonides believed righteous action to be ennobling. In doing so, a person can become more "godlike," if such a thing can be said. The deed itself is its own reward.

Giving, for Maimonides, was one of the highest forms of human behavior. It elevates the soul. It is one of the few ways that human beings can, in a sense, imitate God. God gives to the world unselfishly and generously. God simply gushes over, overflowing with energy that sustains us all. To Maimonides, this kind of divine giving was like "the giving of gifts on the parts of a generous and superior man who does it because of the nobility of his nature and the excellence of his disposition, not because of hope for a reward: this is to become like the deity."[12]

Elsewhere, Maimonides draws a similar analogy to how generosity, both in terms of money and time, connects God and humanity.

Maimonides believed, as was taught by Aristotle, that the universe is governed by "intellects," forces of energy that make nature work and give us life. This divine revelation flows from God through the cosmos to become manifest in us. We, too, can be generous with our energy to those around us.

> Maimonides asks us to imagine an individual who has enough wealth for a residue to be left over from it sufficient for the enrichment of many people, so that this one may give a measure of it to another individual through which this second would also become rich, while a residue is left over from it that suffices for the enrichment of a third individual. The case of being is similar. For the overflow coming from Him, may He be exalted, for the bringing into being of separate intellects overflows likewise from these intellects, so that one of them brings another one into being.[13]

In Maimonides' worldview, we can all enrich each other, both physically and spiritually. Money can be a spiritual tool when it is used in the way that God commands: to protect the vulnerable, to lift people out of poverty, and to spread the blessings of education and peace. Existence itself is a kind of give-and-take, where we share the richness of body and mind and hold each other up. It is through relationships that we see ourselves in the context of something greater.

This idea that being generous gives us meaning and fills us with life also is noted elsewhere in Jewish sacred writing. In the well-known Twenty-third Psalm, the author is filled with gratitude to God for all of the gifts God has given him. Feeling blessed and thankful, he says, "My cup runs over" (Psalm 23:5).

When we feel that our cup runs over, we can believe in our capacity to give. Our overflow, our generosity of spirit, gives us our place in our community and enriches those around us. Overflowing is not sacrifice; it is sharing our fullness. We can only know what this feels like if we risk opening up and sharing what we have to offer.

However, we also can be generous even when we do not necessarily feel that we overflow with blessings. Sometimes performing a generous act is just what we might need to break out of a funk, of the feeling that we have nothing to give. There is dignity and pride in giving to others, and reaching out to someone else in need can release us from thinking only of our own problems. We can feel a kind of high in helping another person. Perhaps this is what the Sages meant when they said, "A poor person who lives on *tzedakah* should give *tzedakah*" (Babylonian Talmud, *Gittin* 7b). Both the giver and the recipient are raised up in spirit.

PUTTING UP WITH THE *SHTUNK* SITTING NEXT TO YOU

Some people are turned off from getting involved in a community because they fear having to sit next to a *shtunk*.

The definition of a *shtunk*: A Yiddish word for someone with a bad odor; also used for a jerk. A loudmouth. The person who is always negative, regardless of the situation. The guy who criticizes not to be helpful but because he enjoys pointing out where others are wrong and he is right. The whiner who talks about how it was once done a certain way and how much better those days were. The one who tantalizes us with rumors, gossip, and secrets, who is more than happy to dish the dirt on another. The person who, try as you might, will not permit you to ignore them, who, out of a group of thirty, somehow hogs everyone's attention.

A great deal can be said about dealing with difficult people that is well beyond the scope of this book. But the simple truth is, it is not always fun to work with other people.

On the other hand, if a community is to be whole, and not an elite club, it must be inclusive. A normal, healthy community includes people we enjoy being around and some we do not. David W. Augsburger explains:

Community, when it is faithful in welcoming its actual members, contains (brace yourself!):

- Contrasts in perspective
- Tensions in relationships
- Ambivalence in motivations
- Variety in preferences
- Diversity in values
- Competition for resources
- Complexities of human needs
- Toxicity in personalities
- Immaturity in development
- —all held together by implicit and explicit contracts, covenants, and the conversations that keep them alive.[14]

The *shtunk* may in fact have been unconsciously assigned that role by a group that feels the need for someone to blame. A tendency of human behavior is the need to finger point. Finding an irritating or immature personality for the group to target is an easy way of passing off group responsibility onto a single person.

Even if not everyone is going to be your best friend, we still need community. We need each other because the sacred work that we do can only be done by a group. Community is too sacred to let a couple of *shtunks* ruin it for everyone else. We need to be tolerant and flexible. The synagogue, in particular, is the place where no one is turned away. The synagogue's doors embrace all. If we believe that this is just, that all people are made in the divine image and should be welcomed into God's house, then we need to accept that *shtunks* are part of the deal.

And who knows? While you're working so hard to be tolerant of others, perhaps someone is dealing with having to put up with you!

"Know Before Whom You Stand"

Men filled with the joy that comes from passionate involvement become leaders in their community. Many people confuse leadership with expertise. A leader, they think, is someone who can tell others what to do in a given situation—someone who knows how a certain kind of business runs, understands a particular system or procedure, or possesses a special knowledge base that can get things done. In Hebrew, such knowledge is referred to as *da'at*. It is a technical kind of knowledge that is very useful and can enhance life.

Leaders, however, do more than offer expert advice. They take their place in the group, surrounded by their community, and they hold to that place. They do not necessarily understand all the details involved in reaching a goal, but they grasp the why. When others react willy-nilly to a situation, they calmly stand their ground. With a combination of insight and equanimity, or what some psychologists call a "nonanxious presence,"[15] leaders hold their own and remain focused on their vision. Leaders know their boundaries, stay within them, and maintain their focus. The Hebrew term for this kind of knowing is *chochmah*. It means "wisdom."

Rabbi Edwin Freedman wrote about the wisdom of leadership this way: Real leadership is not a sacrifice of yourself for the sake of others; neither is it holding yourself high above and being out of touch with the community. Instead, it is a balancing act of self-differentiation and relationship.

Groups, whether they are corporations, congregations, or sports teams, function like a body. Every body needs a leader; the head needs to know that it is the head. It needs to think of itself as a separate entity, different from the rest, with its own boundaries, functions, and needs. At the same time, it must stay in constant touch with the rest of the body to lead.

> If a leader will take primary responsibility for his or her own position as "head" and work to define his or her own goals and self, while *staying in touch* with the rest of the organism, there is a more than reasonable chance that the body will follow.[16]

In other words, in giving time, money, and energy to the community, it is important to set goals and boundaries. We need not immerse ourselves in the needs of others to the point of giving ourselves away, but we do need to be in touch with others to thrive in relationship.

Leadership, therefore, is taking a calm, consistent stand among a group of people to whom you are committed in maintaining a relationship. It is about self and other together, but differentiated.

Jewish men, who historically are part of a people and a history, should not isolate themselves. The result will only be loneliness and restlessness. At the same time, the Jewish people desperately need Jewish men to take leadership roles on their boards and committees. It does not have to mean giving up too much time or losing what you need for yourself. Real leadership is about finding yourself in the midst of a community.

Five Hebrew words, *Da lifnei mi atah omed*, are often found inscribed across the top of the *aron hakodesh*, the ark containing the Torah scrolls in many synagogues. It means, "Know before whom you stand." We stand as individuals before God. We also stand before our communities in front of the congregation. We need a new generation of Jewish men to do both.

Remember the Jewish People

A generation or so ago, North American Jewish men generally joined and contributed volunteer time to organizations with direct ties to the Jewish community. Antisemitism helped explain this phenomenon. Jews simply were not allowed to join many groups dominated by gentiles. However, Jewish men of that era also felt a strong ethnic tie to other Jews, and B'nai B'rith, the American Jewish Committee, Zionist organizations, and other groups were natural group expressions of that identity.

As Jews became more accepted by non-Jews and assimilated, they joined organizations that once banned them. This can also be seen in the world of philanthropy, where Jewish men and women have become leaders in more universal causes in addition to Jewish ones. Today, there is a challenge for Jewish institutions in that Jewish men as a whole are not giving as much as they used to. In addition, when they do give, they are giving less to Jewish causes and more to other kinds of charities. Many Jews today are more likely to give to fight juvenile diabetes, to compensate the victims of 9/11, and to save the rain forest than to support Israel, Jewish Big Brothers & Big Sisters, or Jewish Family and Children's Services. It seems that as our business and technology have become globalized, so has our mindset. For too many, Jewish allegiance is simply antiquated tribalism.

The question is not if other causes or charities are worthwhile. Fighting cancer, addressing genocide, and alleviating hunger are part of our sacred mission. These issues of justice concern us all and are vitally important.

However, an uncomfortable fact of life remains that Jewish men must confront when deciding where to give their time and money. It is simply this: Jews must give to other Jews in order for the Jewish people to survive and thrive. If Jews do not give to Jewish causes—whether it is for soup kitchens or armored ambulances in Israel, elderly poor Jews in the former Soviet Union, or Ethiopian Jews still unable to emigrate—who will? If we do not support Israel or take a stand against antisemitism, who will? If we do not help our fellow congregants in our synagogues, who will?

We need to be both universal and particularistic in our outlook. We need Jewish men to sit on the board of their local hospital as well as serve on a committee at their synagogue. By embracing Jewish causes, we also affirm the historic truth that we Jewish men are part of a collective that has a common purpose, past, and future. We belong to more than just ourselves or humanity in general. *It is a* mitzvah *to share with others and actively support and participate in the life of the Jewish community.*

Community is so basic to Judaism that the entire religious structure would fall apart without it. Judaism is not a privatized spirituality. In contrast to the contemporary rhetoric of the day, Judaism is not first and foremost about "personal journeys," finding our "authentic self," and "private emotional release," although it can give us all these things in wonderful ways.[17] Instead, Judaism is primarily about group responsibility. It is about justice and compassion among the whole, even more than it is about personal enlightenment.

When we pray in Judaism, we do so ideally with a *minyan*, a quorum of Jews necessary to recite all the prayers in their complete form. The default language of prayer in Judaism is "we." We stand before God. We are responsible one for the other. On Yom Kippur we confess our sins as a collective, even for the ones we personally did not commit: "The sin we have committed against You …"[18] We understand every time we take out the Torah that it is a reenactment of when God addressed the Jewish people as a whole on Mount Sinai.

FOR ME, NOT JUST FOR OTHERS

Perhaps the importance of Jewish men taking their place in the community as leaders is best illustrated by a true story. The following is from a letter written by a friend named Stuart, who died recently. A dedicated member of our synagogue, he considered his temple a form of family and his community a "community of caring."

> I write this letter to express to you how much more my Temple family and our community of caring have come to mean to me. Throughout the years, my family has celebrated wonderful events and holidays at the Temple. I took great pleasure in the excitement and exhilaration of my children becoming *b'nei mitzvah* and confirmed as well as having big parties at the Temple…. I had great pride in having had my children educated at the Temple and having had them participate in Chanukah and Passover celebrations in our home. I have been honored by being chosen to sit on the board for many years and serving as President. I cherished meeting and having many congregants as friends over the years. I have watched them age

and saw their children grow up, attending *simchas* in their families. And so much more.

Throughout all of these times, more than thirty years, it has been mostly good times, and largely the concepts of Temple family and a community of caring were paid lip service. It all came so easily without much effort or pain. It was the social place to be and be seen. Occasionally, there were sad times, funerals, illnesses, divorces—but it was always for others, not for me ...

All of that radically changed this past April. From that date, I came to learn the critical importance of Temple family and a community of caring. Last spring, I was diagnosed with a rare form of thyroid cancer and had major surgery as well as significant treatment and care. I am having my last radiation treatment tomorrow morning.

Throughout this ordeal, the Temple and its members have provided me with much emotional support and encouragement. My friends, developed from my association with the Temple, have been there for me with reassuring cards, pats on the back, telephone calls and visits, books to read, donations in my honor, ice cream to eat, encouraging comments, and inquiries expressing interest and concern. I have seen these outpourings for others over the years and never believed that I would ever need such benefits. You know, we are all so indestructible— until we are not ...

My hope is that others never experience what I have in order to fully understand and appreciate the meaning and importance of a community of caring.[19]

A synagogue is a *kehilah kedoshah,* a "sacred community." The word "sacred" means that it is of ultimate importance, the place where we go that is at the heart of everything. Sacred communities are not just the places we give to. You may find yourself receiving more than you can imagine.

QUESTIONS FOR REFLECTION

- What are some of the reasons people join synagogues? What are some of the reasons people do not join?

- What opportunities for *tzedakah* (charity or "righteous giving") move you? Are there opportunities for *gemilut chasadim* (volunteerism)?

- Do you feel an obligation to help the Jewish community in particular? Why or why not?

- Do you believe Jewish giving to non-Jewish causes is reciprocated by non-Jews giving to Jewish causes?

- Name five Jewish causes that also aid non-Jews.

- Why do you think Judaism puts such a strong emphasis on community? What does a sense of community offer people?

7

The *Mitzvot* of Manhood

The fruit of the righteous is a tree of life; a wise man captivates people. (Proverbs 11:30)

At all stages of life, we need role models. There is a Chasidic story that illustrates this idea, a story about a Sage so famous for his ability to tell tales and to capture an audience that he was called the Maggid, "the Teller."

The story goes that a young student sat with his teacher in a private moment. The student asked his teacher if it was true that the teacher's teacher had been the Maggid.

"Yes, it is true."

"What was it like to hear the famous teacher tell a story?" the student asks.

"It was magical. I traveled a great distance to be able to study at that wise man's feet. It was a difficult and dangerous journey, but it was worth it. But in truth, I did not travel so long and hard and risk myself just to hear the man's stories."

"Then why did you go?"

"I wanted to see everything he did, to learn from the man and his life. I wanted to watch how he ate and drank, how he spoke to his wife, and how he played with his children. I wanted to see him cover his mouth when he coughed or sneezed. I wanted to see how he tied his shoes."[1]

The teacher's deepest learning took place not in listening to a discourse, but in finding someone to emulate, down to the mundane act of how he tied his shoes. We all look for teachers who can mentor us.

There is a different, and rather humorous, story in the Talmud of a student who was so zealous about learning from his rabbi's actions that he hid under his teacher's bed. When his teacher began to make love with his wife, the hidden student muttered something to himself in amazement, giving himself away. A chaotic scene erupted. "This too is Torah," the student protested, "and I need to learn!" (Babylonian Talmud, *Berachot* 62a).

We must recognize that just as we seek role models, we are role models to others, whether we like it or not. I am personally reminded of this when my children watch me shave, which is something they take delight in. My daughter stands at one side of the sink and my son on the other. They stare in fascination at the mirror each morning as I slowly remove the shaving cream with a razor. Such moments remind me that they are always watching me, even when I do not realize it. All children watch what we do, and they seem to absorb everything—for good and for bad.

THE *CHACHAM*, NOT THE *CHASID*

Moses Maimonides took the idea of Jewish men as role models very seriously. In fact, in his investigations into Jewish sacred literature, he identified two different paradigms as to how to be a spiritual Jewish man.

The first paradigm is the figure of the *chasid*, which translates as the "devout" or "pious." Some go as far as to understand the *chasid* as a "saint." The *chasid* is extreme in his generosity and piety. Jewish sources tell us that a genuine *chasid* practices, "What's mine is yours, and what's yours is yours." The *chasid* not only gives to charity but inspires others to do so, too. He goes to the synagogue to learn, and he puts what he learns into practice. In temperament, he is slow to anger and easy to calm (*Pirkei Avot* 5:10–14). He arrives at the synagogue early to meditate for an hour in preparation for prayer (*Mishnah Berachot* 5:1). He goes beyond the letter of the law and stays far from even the perception of transgression. The *chasid* willingly takes on extra fasts and other forms of self-denial to hone his humble demeanor (*Shemonah Perakim* 4:3).

Modern-day examples of the *chasid* abound. They need not be Jews; consider, for example, such well-known figures as Mahatma Gandhi, Mother Teresa, or the Dalai Lama. I can also think of contemporaries who demand as much of others as they demand of themselves; perfectionists go to extremes to make everything right. Such people are often never satisfied because they're always seeking to do more and to do better. Often they are looked upon as role models, and they may accomplish much good in the world. But sometimes their standards are impossibly high for others. We seem never to be as "good" as they are.

It is perhaps for this reason that Maimonides chose to focus on a second kind of figure to emulate. This figure is the *chacham* or "wise man." Whereas the *chasid* strives for perfection, the *chacham* aspires for balance.

> Good acts are those midway between two extremes that are bad, namely, excess and absence.
> Prudence, for example, is midway between excessive desire and its absence....
> Generosity is midway between miserliness and extravagance.
> Courage is midway between recklessness and cowardice.
> Self-confidence is midway between arrogance and debasement.
> Dignity is midway between being overbearing and being obsequious....
> Humility is midway between pride and shame.[2]

Virtue, Maimonides taught, is found in the middle path. Excess in any direction is not healthy. Sometimes we need to go to an extreme temporarily to counterbalance a deficiency. But the ideal is to be found in moderation (*Shemonah Perakim* 4:3). Maimonides wrote, "In truth, it is the middle way that should be praised" (*Shemonah Perakim* 4:2).[3] Just as Maimonides advised "the golden mean" for emotional characteristics, so is it with physical health. He counseled that we should eat and drink when we are hungry and thirsty, not out of boredom or for any other reason. He recommended daily exercise and sleeping eight hours each night. "A man should aim to maintain physical health and vigor, in order that his soul may be upright, in a condition to know God," he wrote (*Hilchot De'ot* 4).[4] Maimonides was a physician; his advice sounds just like the advice my doctor gives me today.

We all know what we must do to enhance our chances for optimum physical, emotional, and spiritual health. Yet it's hard to break bad habits. Judaism teaches that physical and emotional self-care is necessary for our spiritual well-being. One's body is a gift from God that should be treated with respect and given the sense of balance it deserves. With healthy habits of diet, exercise, and sleep, Maimonides taught that we can prevent a good deal of illness. The purpose of physical and emotional balance, according to Maimonides, is to enable us to pursue wisdom and be a *chacham*. It is only in a condition of physical and emotional health that we can have an "upright soul" and can "know God." Greater intellectual and spiritual heights can be achieved only with a healthy foundation.

WORK, WORK, WORKAHOLIC

Maintaining a healthy balance is difficult, particularly when the surrounding culture pressures you to do otherwise. Western culture pressures men to work, and then to work some more. The more time spent at work, the more we are rewarded. I often hear about bosses who pay lip service to employees taking vacation time in the interest of "a balanced life," yet somehow they themselves never take time off. What a double message. Who feels comfortable taking a vacation when the boss doesn't? Who is able to truly rest on a vacation when all you can think of is the catching up that's required when you return to the job? It's a treadmill, only to be perpetuated when you the employee eventually become the boss habituated to maintaining the same unhealthy pattern. We talk about family and spirituality, but we do not reward it.

Jewish men are in great need of a model of balance at work. The problem is an old one, but men can find appropriate mentors to guide them. For example, if we return to the relationship between Moses and his father-in-law, Jethro, we can learn an important survival skill—the ability to delegate. The story goes something like this (Exodus 18:13–24):

Moses has been working very hard to serve his people. Before he finishes breakfast, a line has formed outside his tent. He is not just the leader of his people. He is also their personal adviser. He sits in front of them, and each presents their concerns. Two people have issues about the values of their livestock and the price of chickens. Another person does not know if his ailing mother should live in his family's tent or her own. Still another wants to know when they will get to the Promised Land because his feet are beginning to hurt and he's not sure his donkey will make it much longer. By midmorning, the line to see Moses stretches around the tent, down the corner, and right out of camp. Moses, bleary-eyed, handles one problem after another as fast as he can, while managing to give each individual his personal, undivided attention.

Along comes Moses's father-in-law, Jethro, who cannot believe his eyes. The line of people is growing and growing. People are camping out the night before in order to secure a good spot in line. He even catches one person scalping tickets.

"Moses!" Jethro interrupts. "This is no good! You're tired of sitting. They're tired of standing, and my daughter and grandchildren are being neglected. This system isn't working for anybody. Eventually, you're going to kill yourself if you keep this up. Instead, why don't you appoint district courts, superior courts, and then eventually a Supreme Court. The small cases can go to the district courts, and the bigger ones can go up the ladder. You and God can be the Supreme Court. You cannot do this by yourself; let other people help you. What do you say?"

Moses agrees, and everyone is much happier.

The story's point should be obvious: Moses feels overly responsible for addressing the people's concerns to the point of micromanaging everyone's affairs. The people come to him, and he has no idea how to say "no." After all, don't the people deserve the wisdom that he has to offer? Shouldn't he help if he can? Moses's role model and mentor, Jethro, teaches that this is well-meaning but destructive behavior. "You cannot do it alone," Jethro cautions. It is not only that it is unhealthy for Moses; it is also unhealthy for the people. Moses is tired, but the people are wearied as well. "Let them share the burden with you," Jethro advises. Moses follows his father-in-law's advice and creates a hierarchy so that the work can be done with more ease and efficiency. More importantly, it creates an opportunity to *not work*.

For many, not working has become an incredibly difficult activity. Cell phones, pagers, and e-mail have created the expectation that we should be available all the time. The new technology binds us to the workplace. The expectation is that we will respond to an e-mail the same day if not the same hour it is received. Such expectations were unknown a generation ago. Contemporary culture dictates that to be "responsible" means to always be ready to work. Nothing, however, could be more irresponsible.

For some reason, workaholism—the state of obsessively and compulsively working to the detriment of relationships, outside interests, and health—seems an acceptable addiction today. It is for this reason that one physician calls it the "respectable" addiction. Dr. Bryan Robinson, author of *Chained to the Desk*[5] explained when interviewed, "Hard work put us on the moon and discovered vaccinations and built this country. But hard workers generally have some balance in their lives. They sit at their desks and think about skiing. The workaholic is on the ski slopes thinking about work."[6]

As with any addiction, stopping requires a spiritual solution. The constant use of electronic toys feeds the expectation of instant gratification and results. Just as members of Alcoholics Anonymous admit they are powerless to stop drinking without help from a Higher Power, so must we seek out spiritual relationships and mentoring to help us live lives of balance. It's no surprise that AA spawned Workaholics Anonymous. "Workaholics Anonymous is a fellowship of individuals who share their experience, strength, and hope with each other that they may solve their common problems and help others to recover from workaholism."[7]

Judaism's Antidote to Workaholism

Jews are fortunate. God anticipated workaholism. High up on our list of commandments is the directive to keep Shabbat. Needless to say, the Israelites never had the weekend off as slaves in Egypt. But then God gave them a radical directive—rest. It was not an option; it was a commandment for their survival. One rabbi once told me that the only people who burn out are the people who set themselves on fire.[8] We all need Shabbat for our own revitalization.

Jewish men need to help make Shabbat happen in their homes. Their families need it, and they need it. The first step can be as simple as a two-minute ritual on Friday night and the insistence that the family be together for a weekly family meal. The dinner does not have to be elaborate; pizza will do. It's okay to stammer through the blessings over the candles, wine, and bread. God understands us. The essence of the moment is togetherness, reflection, and celebration. It is about flicking a switch in our brains so that we enter a different mindset. It is about renewal.

Judaism is not about finding God in the extremes of life, on mountaintops, or in dangerous thrills. Judaism is about finding God within the ordinary, in something as simple as a loaf of bread. It's about recognizing the miracle of everyday life. It takes just minutes to say the blessings for Shabbat on Friday night, but it can be transformative. It is even more so when you get in the habit of saying the blessings every Friday night, week after week. The secret to renewal and togetherness is regularity and consistency. Just a two-minute discipline, done weekly, can make our children eager and excited about this sacred time. The philosopher Ahad Ha'am is quoted as saying, "More than Israel has kept the Sabbath has the Sabbath kept Israel."

If your identity is all about work, it can be liberating to define yourself through family at the Shabbat dinner table and by participating in a synagogue service. The *Kiddush*, or blessing over the wine, on Friday night contains the essence of a different way of seeing ourselves: we take a moment "to recall our liberation from Egypt." Slavery in Egypt can be a metaphor for endless routines, a demanding office, or a frantic mind. It is a central commandment that we stop once a week, whatever our initial resistance. Cease and you are free.

In his classic book of modern Jewish spirituality, *The Sabbath*, Rabbi Abraham Joshua Heschel talks of this form of liberation that is so necessary for Jewish men today: "The Sabbath is not for the sake of the weekdays; the weekdays are for the sake of the Sabbath. It is not an interlude but the climax of living."[9]

Work can be fulfilling, but it ought not be your ultimate fulfillment. *It is a* mitzvah *to live a life of balance, not sinning at the idol of endless work and productivity.*

People need to reach out to each other. We need to go on this journey together. Life is not something that can be done alone. In all areas of life, whether it be work or otherwise, men need relationships in their family and community to be healthy. In need of inspiration? Just ask yourself what it is you are modeling for the next generation.

Students Become Teachers

I find it thrilling that a student can become a teacher. Where we once were mentored, we have the privilege of helping another. Moses is counseled by Jethro, and Moses, in turn, becomes a teacher.

Moses's successor, Joshua, has the difficult task of leading the people after him. At the end of his life, Moses is not qualified to lead the Israelite army into the Land of Israel. A younger man is required for the job. Joshua is that younger man; however, being younger also means he has less experience. Moses offers him support and encouragement. He calls him up in front of the people and says, "Be strong and resolute!" More than that, he encourages him and tells him that God "will be with you; God will not fail you or forsake you. Fear not and be not dismayed!" (Deuteronomy 31:7–8).

We might imagine that Moses sees a reflection of himself in the young Joshua. In soothing Joshua's fear, Moses is remembering himself.

We make our own way in the world, but we do so with the help of others. A central Jewish prayer teaches us this lesson. In the first blessing of the *T'filah*, literally "the Prayer" when we each stand before God, we invoke the Almighty as "our God and the God of our ancestors." Why must we invoke God both as our personal God as well as the God of our fathers and mothers? The Baal Shem Tov, the Chasidic master, explains that these phrases represent two types of faith. The phrase "our God" represents the faith we acquire through our experience. It is a personal kind of faith we arrive at independently through our own reflection. Another kind of faith is contained in the phrase "our fathers and mothers." This faith has come to us from tradition, from our role models and teachers.

However, a personal faith can be proven wrong, and a tradition can be inherited unthinkingly. It is therefore necessary to combine both kinds of faith, faith that is handed down and faith that we arrive at on our own, for the strongest possible relationship with God.[10]

One of the central tasks of being a Jewish man is to pass the covenant to the next generation. We do so not in one dramatic moment, but in small, everyday actions. Students become teachers, and we relearn faith. We receive and pass the covenant in how we behave as sons, partners in marriage, fathers, and leaders in our community. We inherit wisdom, add our insights to it, and then transmit it, so it is not lost. From generation to generation, there is inevitable and often enormous change, but there is also renewal.

RENEWING THE COVENANT: THE *MITZVOT* OF MANHOOD

"To be a man is, precisely, to be responsible."[11]

A father brings his son forward for circumcision traditionally on the eighth day of the boy's life. This ceremony, called a *b'rit*, literally means "covenant." A covenant is about responsibility; one Jewish man brings up another. This ceremony is one of many acts of covenant making.

What are Jewish men responsible for at the beginning of the twenty-first century? In the spirit of the eighth day, here are eight tasks toward renewing the covenant for Jewish men:

- To seek Jewish wisdom, informed by both tradition and our own unique relationship with God, freed from stereotypes of Jewish men
- To name our fathers for who they really were during our growing up even as we commit to honoring our parents
- To be "a matching helper" to our partners in marriage and not define ourselves solely as providers and breadwinners
- To be compassionate fathers, stepfathers, or mentors toward children and not defined only as disciplinarians but also as men strong enough to demonstrate love
- To be role models of Torah in word and deed and, whenever possible, to personally teach Torah to our children
- To forgive others and ourselves, living up to God's expectations of "very good" and not "perfect"
- To be generous while supporting and actively participating in the life of the Jewish community
- To live a life of balance rather than worshiping the idol of endless work and productivity

OUT OF HIDING

In James B. Twitchell and Ken Ross's fascinating book *Where Men Hide*, the authors admit that a better title might have been "Where Men Hid."[12] The book is a collection of photographs and articles about places that were once numerous but are now disappearing, places that are for "men only." These are places where men used to go to be with other men (and often to escape the company of women)—the fraternal lodge, the barbershop, and the room reserved for the man of the house to retreat to with his pipe. Some places are now shared with women and have thus lost their "men only" quality—the baseball dugout no longer has photos of scantily clad women tacked to its walls, because the space is now shared with the girls' softball team. The book's photographs are dark and have a dreary quality, for the landscape of men's space has declined. In Twitchell's words, "Mars has shrunk."[13]

The synagogue is no exception. With the disposal in liberal synagogues of the *mechitza,* the traditional barrier that separated men and women during prayer, the synagogue has become a place that men and women share.

Given the world's and Judaism's history of oppressive patriarchy, some may feel men are no longer entitled to their own domain or even that they need permission from women before getting together with other men, as if they might do something wrong. Men coming together to be with other men, however, is as natural as women being with other women. It is about commonality and understanding. But younger Jewish men seem not to be seeking out this experience.

Where are the young men? Many are seated in front of computers or playing video games. Others download music and listen to it alone, closed off to the world by earphones. It is true that some young Jewish men are more fully sharing their lives with women than in the past. It should be so, for the subjugation of women has lasted far too long. We are all benefiting from having

50 percent of the population giving their intellect and talent toward Jewish life.

In contrast to Jewish men, however, women seem able to create both mixed-gender spaces and women-only spaces. The woman who attends a mixed-gender class and participates in services also goes to her women's book club, mahjong game, or Rosh Chodesh group (celebrating the monthly cycle of the Jewish lunar calendar). Men, however, seem to spend time in mixed-gender company and alone, but not with each other. For men in their thirties and forties, the concept of brotherhood or a male-only space outside of competitive sports seems foreign. But too many have become solitary creatures who seek comfort in mouse clicks and keyboard strokes.[14] At work they inhabit walled-off cubicles and closed-door offices. Such isolation is a tragedy.

Nor does it satisfy our need for meaning and community—needs that must be addressed to lead a fulfilling and happy life. We can satisfy our craving for meaning and community within our heritage. We can redefine Jewish men's spirituality on our own terms. However, for Jewish men to fulfill our potential we must seek each other out. Instead of men's hiding places, why not unapologetically create new spaces in the open?

One of these spaces should be the synagogue, which is not so much a new space as it can be rejuvenated space. Make it a place where men come together to study Judaism and learn about themselves and each other in the different roles we play from birth to death.

My synagogue holds a monthly men's study group, where we meet and talk about many of the passages that have been referenced in these pages. Many of us read these stories as children but have not encountered them since. In reading the stories from the Torah and the Talmud as adults, we discover something intriguing. We discover something we did not realize we were missing: spiritual, intellectual, and emotional enrichment. Many in the group rearrange schedules to get their monthly "fix" of Jewish learning. In the words of one participant: "Before, I was just a member here for High Holy Day tickets and my daughter's bat mitzvah. I now realize that there is something for me as well."

My synagogue is not unique. What we do can easily be replicated by your synagogue. You can find sacred space for men through men's study groups and other programs. If you do not belong to a synagogue, try one or two out or share this book with a brother, father, son, or other relative or friend and see what he thinks. In doing so, you take a step toward renewing the covenant of Israel and creating healthier families and communities. It is not too ambitious to say that men cultivating wisdom in the highest spirit of Jewish tradition is a step toward healing the larger world as well.

Notes

Chapter 2: Beyond Portnoy

1. National Jewish Population Survey 2000–2001, United Jewish Communities, 2003, http://www.ujc.org/content_display.html?ArticleID=83794.
2. U.S. Department of Labor Women's Bureau, "Employment Status of Women and Men in 2005," http://www.dol.gov/wb/factsheets/Qf-ESWM05.htm.
3. U.S. Department of Labor Bureau of Labor Statistics, "Men's and Women's Work Hours, 2005," http://www.bls.gov/opub/ted/2006/oct/wk1/art03.htm.
4. Peter Kuhn and Fernanco Lozano, "The Expanding Workweek? Understanding Trends in Long Work Hours among U.S. Men, 1979–2004," *National Bureau of Economic Research*, Working Paper No. 11895, December 2005, http://papers.nber.org/papers/w11895.
5. Alan E. Pisarski, *Commuting in America III: The Third National Report on Commuting Patterns and Trends* (Washington, DC: Transportation Research Board, 2006), 46–59.
6. Judith S. Wallerstein and Sandra Blakeslee, *The Good Marriage: How and Why Love Lasts* (New York: Warner Books, 1995), 161.
7. Esther Dermott, "Dads Want Flexibility, Not Shorter Worker Hours," *Medical News Today*, August 25, 2006, http://www.medicalnewstoday.com/medicalnews.php?newsid=50384.
8. Doug Barden, *Wrestling with Jacob and Esau, Fighting the Flight of Men: A Modern Day Crisis for the Reform Movement* (New York: North American Federation of Temple Brotherhoods, 2005), 11–13.
9. Ibid.
10. Steven E. Rhoads, *Taking Sex Differences Seriously* (San Francisco: Encounter Books, 2004), 150.
11. This is not an isolated phenomenon. In religious movements all across the nation, not just in Judaism, there has been a noticeable decline in the attendance and involvement of men. Unitarian, Lutheran, Episcopalian, Methodist, Congregational, Presbyterian, and Roman Catholic

church publications all have been recently asking the question as to where the men have gone from their pews. In addition, traditional secular men's groups, such as lodges and the Masons, have an aging population with few young members to replace them. See Barden, *Wrestling with Jacob and Esau*, 11–17, 46–48.

12. Philip Roth, *Portnoy's Complaint* (New York: Vintage International, 1994), 245, 269.
13. See, for instance, Matthew Biberman, *Masculinity, Antisemitism, and Early Modern English Literature: From the Satanic to the Effeminate Jew* (Aldershot, Hampshire: Ashgate Publishing, 2004).
14. Jay Geller, "The Godfather of Psychoanalysis: Circumcision, Antisemitism, Homosexuality, and Freud's 'Fighting Jew,'" *Journal of American Academy of Religion*, no. 2 (1999): 355–86.
15. D. S. Katz, "Shylock's Gender: Jewish Male Menstruation in Early Modern England," in *The Review of English Studies* (Oxford: Oxford University Press, 1999), 440–62.
16. Sigmund Freud, *The Interpretation of Dreams*, trans. James Strachey (New York: Avon Books, 1998), 230. Originally published in 1900.
17. This passage is featured in Daniel Boyarin, *Unheroic Conduct: The Rise of Heterosexuality and the Invention of the Jewish Man* (Berkeley: University of California Press, 1997), 33, and is the inspiration for the title of that work.
18. Otto Weininger, *Sex and Character* (New York: G. P. Putnam's Sons, 1907), 306.
19. See also Andrea Dworkin, "The Sexual Mythology of Antisemitism," in *A Mensch among Men: Explorations in Jewish Masculinity*, ed. Harry Brod (Freedom, Calif.: Crossing Press, 1988), 118–23.
20. Theodor Lessing, "Jewish Self-Hatred [1930]," in *The Jew in the Modern World*, eds. Paul Mendes-Flohr and Jehuda Reinharz (Oxford: Oxford University Press, 1995), 272.
21. Haim Nahman Bialik, "The City of Slaughter [1903]" in Mendes-Flohr and Reinharz, *Jew in the Modern World*, 410–11.
22. Jeffrey K. Salkin, *Searching for My Brothers: Jewish Men in a Gentile World* (New York: G. P. Putnam's Sons, 1999), 71.
23. Ibid., 73, 81, 99.
24. See Genesis Rabbah 63:6, 10, 12, 14.
25. For example, see Babylonian Talmud, *Gittin* 57b.
26. For example, see Ibid., *Pesachim* 56a.
27. Henry E. Kagan, lecture delivered at UAHC Biennial, Chicago, November 16, 1963, cited in W. Gunther Plaut and David E. S. Stein, eds., *The Torah: A Modern Commentary*, rev. ed. (New York: Union for Reform Judaism, 2005), 187.
28. When asked by a college student, "Why are all Jewish guys wusses?" Rabbi Salkin answered, "It's not that Jewish men are wusses. It's that our code

of masculinity is simply different. We demonstrate our masculinity through a love of ideas and words, an infatuation with argument and intellectual striving. Some people think that to be a man you have to know how to go it alone. Not Jewish men. We live like men in the midst of a community, showing responsibility and living lives of interconnection. Some people think that to be a man is to 'do what you gotta do.' Not Jewish men. We show that we are men through a strict adherence to a moral code. It means lifting ourselves higher than we ever thought possible." See Salkin, *Searching for My Brothers*, 34, 67–68.

29. Ibid., 3.
30. Indeed, the cultural assumption of masculine as assertive and feminine as passive has much of its origin in Roman imperial history. See Boyarin, *Unheroic Conduct*, 5–6.
31. See Rich Cohen, *Tough Jews: Fathers, Sons, and Gangster Dreams* (New York: Random House, 1999).
32. National Jewish Population Survey 2000–2001, United Jewish Communities, 2003, http://www.ujc.org/content_display.html?ArticleID=83911.
33. Samuel Osherson, *Finding Our Fathers* (New York: Contemporary Books, 2001), 168–70.
34. This teaching was pointed out to me by Rabbi Gustav Buchdahl.
35. Steven Z. Leder, "God's Loneliest Creatures," http://menweb.org/leder.htm.
36. Henry David Thoreau, "Economy," in *Walden: Or, Life in the Woods* (New York: Penguin Groups USA, 1980), 10.
37. Robert Moore and Douglas Gillette, *King, Warrior, Magician, Lover: Rediscovering the Archetypes of the Mature Masculine* (San Francisco: HarperCollins Publishers, 1990), 13.
38. One can be agnostic and still be grounded in Jewish traditional values as represented by fulfilling *mitzvot*, divine commandments. While religiously this is not ideal, it is nevertheless a fact that more secular Jews like Albert Einstein were culturally Jewish and committed to a Jewish sense of education and intellectual pursuit.
39. For a comprehensive list and for statistics on Jewish Nobel Prize winners, see http://www.jinfo.org/Nobel_Prizes.html.

CHAPTER 3: GROWING UP AND BEING A SON

1. From a confidential interview.
2. When Potiphar's wife demanded that Joseph lie with her, the Talmud says that his father's face appeared to him and asked him if he was ready to give up his legacy for this moment of pleasure. It is at that moment that Joseph's passion subsided.

3. Judith Viorst, *Necessary Losses: The Loves, Illusions, Dependencies, and Impossible Expectations That All of Us Have to Give Up in Order to Grow* (New York: Fawcett Columbine Books, 1986), 64.

4. Ibid., 156–57.

5. Moore and Gillette, *King, Warrior, Magician, Lover*, 24–26.

6. Ibid., 37–42.

7. Ibid., 118.

8. In Judaism, each person has an impulse for evil and an impulse for good. This source tells us that the impulse to evil is at least thirteen years older than the impulse for good, for it is not until the time of bar or bat mitzvah that a child matures into a civilized human being who is morally responsible.

9. Susan Morris Shaffer and Linda Perlman Gordan, *Why Boys Don't Talk and Why We Care* (Chevy Chase, Md.: Mid-Atlantic Equity Consortium, 2000), 43.

10. Ibid., 136–37.

11. This is an abbreviated version of Lord Raglan's list of twenty-two points of the myth of the hero. Lord Raglan, "The Hero: A Study in Tradition, Myth, and Drama, Part II," in *In Quest of the Hero* (Princeton, N.J.: Princeton University Press, 1990), 138.

12. Carl Jung, "The Phenomenology of the Spirit in Fairytales," in *The Archetypes and the Collective Unconscious* (Princeton, N.J.: Princeton University Press, 1959), 215–18.

13. Osherson, *Finding Our Fathers*, 3.

14. Ibid., 18.

15. Ibid., 25.

16. Ibid., 49.

17. Ibid., 28–40.

18. In Plaut and Stein, *The Torah*, 142.

19. "[One form of perfection] consists in the individual's moral habits having attained their ultimate excellence. Most of the commandments serve no other end than the attainment of this species of perfection." Moses Maimonides, *The Guide of the Perplexed*, transl. Shlomo Pines (Chicago: University of Chicago Press, 1963), III: 54, 635.

20. A song by Moshe Yess, "My Zayde," illustrates beautifully the sentiment of who this kind of grandfather once was and our responsibility to imagine ourselves as one day being grandfathers.

CHAPTER 4: GROWING UP AND BEING A PARTNER IN MARRIAGE

1. For example, see *Hidushei Aggadot* I, *Kol Kitvei Maharal*, or Rabbi Samson Raphael Hirsch on Genesis 17:15.

2. See Maurice Lamm, *The Jewish Way in Love and Marriage* (New York: Jonathan David Publishers, 1991), 199–206.

3. This text was authored by Rabbi Gustav Buchdahl, Rabbi Lawrence Kushner, and Rabbi Bernard H. Mehlman.

4. Wallerstein and Blakeslee, *Good Marriage*, 211.

5. Ibid., 213.

6. In 2007, www.salary.com estimated the annual value of a full-time mother's work at $138,095. A second-shift mother's work was estimated to be $85,939 in addition to her day job. See http://www.salary.com/site-search/layoutscripts/sisl_display.asp?filename=&path=/destinationsearch/personal/par642_body.html.

7. Wallerstein and Blakeslee, *Good Marriage*, 22.

8. Ibid., 154–56.

9. Ibid., 156.

10. Rashi on Genesis 2:18.

11. See Arthur Waskow, *Down-to-Earth Judaism: Food, Money, Sex, and the Rest of Life* (New York: William Morrow and Company, 1995), 247.

12. Nelson Mandela, *Long Walk to Freedom* (Boston: Little, Brown and Company, 1994), 544.

13. L. A. McKeown, "Breadwinner Anxiety: Man's New Worry," *WebMD Medical News*, June 27, 2001, http://www.webmd.com/content/article/33/1728_82401.htm.

14. "How We Work: Working Women Do More Chores Than Men," Associated Press, September 15, 2004, as reported by www.msnbc.msn.com/id/6011245/.

15. Viorst, *Necessary Losses*, 198.

16. Steven E. Rhoads, *Taking Sex Differences Seriously* (San Francisco: Encounter Books, 2004), 27–34.

17. Bestsellers include John Gray, *Men Are from Mars, Women Are from Venus* (New York: HarperCollins Publishers, 1992), and Deborah Tannen, *You Just Don't Understand: Women and Men in Conversation* (New York: HarperCollins Publishers, 1992).

18. Rhoads, *Taking Sex Differences Seriously*, 32–34.

19. Erina L. MacGeorge, "The Myth of Gender Cultures: Similarities Outweigh Differences in Men's and Women's Provision of and Responses to Supportive Communication," *Sex Roles: A Journal of Research*, February 2004, http://findarticles.com/p/articles/mi_m2294/is_3-4_50/ai_114703688.

20. Gray, *Men Are from Mars, Women Are from Venus*.

21. Kenneth Wenning, *Men Are from Earth, Women Are from Earth: A Guide to Winning Cooperation from Your Spouse* (Northvale, N.J.: Jason Aronson, 1998).

22. Calvin S. Hall and Vernon J. Nordby, *A Primer of Jungian Psychology* (New York: Penguin Books USA, 1973), 46–48.

23. Joel Lurie Grishaver, *The Bonding of Isaac* (Los Angeles: Alef Design Group, 1997), 6.

24. Ibid., 44.

25. Ibid., 43–44.

26. Daniel Chanan Matt, *Zohar: The Book of Enlightenment* (Mahwah, N.J.: Paulist Press, 1983), 55–56. See also Matt's critical translation, Daniel C. Matt, *The Zohar* (Stanford, Calif.: Stanford University Press, 2004), 1: 313–14.

27. Gershom Scholem, *Kabbalah* (Jerusalem: Keter Publishing House, 1974), 317–18.

28. Ibid., 105–16; and Daniel Matt, *The Essential Kabbalah* (Edison, N.J.: Castle Books, 1997), 1–13.

29. Joseph Gikatilla, *Sha'arei Orah* 19a–b, in Matt, *Essential Kabbalah*, 79.

30. The Sages base this on Exodus 21:10.

31. *Hilchot Ishut*, 14:1. The translation used here comes from Isaac Klein, *The Code of Maimonides Book Four: The Book of Women* (New Haven: Yale University Press, 1972), 87.

32. *Iggeret Hakodesh* 2. The translation used here comes from Seymour J. Cohen, *The Holy Letter: A Study in Jewish Sexual Morality* (Northvale, N.J.: Jason Aronson, 1993), 72.

33. *Hilchot Ishut* 15:17–18, in Klein, *Code of Maimonides*, 97–98.

34. *Iggeret Hakodesh* 6, in Cohen, *Holy Letter*, 172.

35. Brad E. Sachs, *The Good Enough Child: How to Have an Imperfect Family and Be Perfectly Satisfied* (New York: HarperCollins Publishers, 2001), 274.

36. Wallerstein and Blakeslee, *Good Marriage*, 27–28.

37. The Jeff Herman Resource Center of the Hebrew Union College–Jewish Institute of Religion in Los Angeles has a large number of online resources concerning gay marriage, liturgy, and counseling. There are also resources for parents of gay children. See http://www.huc.edu/IJSO/. Also, for an example of a wedding program for a gay wedding that addresses some of these issues, see Paul Horowitz and Scott Klein, "A Ceremony of Commitment," in *Twice Blessed: On Being Lesbian, Gay, and Jewish*, ed. Christie Balka and Andy Rose (Boston: Beacon Press, 1989), 126–27.

38. During the Middle Ages, Moses Maimonides was among very few legal authorities to openly condone striking one's wife. Others offered a mix of apologetics and evasiveness on the issue. In Germany, where women had a high social status, we can find rejections of such behavior. In modern times, Jewish authorities of all movements and denominations have universally condemned such violence. See Elliot N. Dorff, *Love Your Neighbor as Yourself: A Jewish Approach to Modern Personal Ethics* (Philadelphia: Jewish Publication Society, 2003), 159–66.

39. Joseph Karo, *Beit Yosef* to the *Tur, Even Ha'ezer* 154:15, as cited in Dorff, *Love Your Neighbor*, 162.

40. Bob Gluck, "Jewish Men and Violence in the Home—Unlikely Companions?" in *A Mensch among Men: Explorations in Jewish Masculinity*, ed. Harry Brod (Freedom, Calif.: Crossing Press, 1988), 163–64.

41. Ibid., 164.

42. Ibid., 165.

43. There is currently no national website for Batterers Anonymous. They can be reached at Batterers Anonymous, c/o Dr. Jerry Goffman, 1040 South Mount Vernon Avenue G-306, Colton, Calif. 92324.

44. For more information, see the JACS website: www.jacsweb.org.

45. For the Awareness Center, see www.theawarenesscenter.org. For Jewish Women International, see www.jwi.org. For Jewish Social Services, see the Association of Jewish Family and Children's Agencies at www.ajfca.org.

46. *Rabbi's Manual* (New York: Central Conference of American Rabbis, 1988), 56.

Chapter 5: Growing Up and Being a Father

1. Sachs, *Good Enough Child*, 221.

2. James T. Bond, Ellen Galinsky, Stacy S. Kim, and Erin Brownfield, *National Study of Employers 2005*, Family and Work Institute, 2–3, http://familiesandwork.org/summary/2005nsesummary.pdf.

3. Brad Sachs, *Blind Date* (Baltimore: Chestnut Hills Press, 1992), 38.

4. Wendy Mogel, *The Blessing of a Skinned Knee* (New York: Penguin Books, 2001), 91.

5. The term is popularly used in the media, such as by Stephanie Armour, "'Helicopter' Parents Hover When Kids Job Hunt," *USA Today*, April 23, 2007, http://www.usatoday.com/money/economy/employment/2007-04-23-helicopter-parents-usat_N.htm.

6. Mogel, *Blessing of a Skinned Knee*, 90–92.

7. Chaim I. Waxman, "The Jewish Father: Past and Present," in *A Mensch among Men: Explorations in Jewish Masculinity*, ed. Harry Brod (Freedom, Calif.: Crossing Press, 1988), 60–61.

8. Ibid., 63.

9. Ibid., 64.

10. Ibid., 67.

11. Ibid., 60.

12. Ibid., 71.

13. Mogel, *Blessing of a Skinned Knee*, 113.

14. From the prayers *Avinu Malkeinu* and *Hayom Harat Olam* in the High Holy Day prayer book in the Rosh Hashanah service. For the sake of gender sensitivity, many prayer books today simply retain the Hebrew, *Avinu Malkeinu*, rather than translate it as "our Father, our King."

15. Recited on the eve of Yom Kippur, this abbreviated version of the prayer comes from Chaim Stern, ed., *Gates of Repentance* (New York: Central Conference of American Rabbis, 1978), 279.

16. This story, taken from Lamentations Rabbah 4:14 and Ecclesiastes Rabbah 10:20, was taught to me by Joel Lurie Grishaver during a conference in Troy, Michigan, in 1997. He ingeniously combined the stories.

17. Sachs, *Good Enough Child*, 14–35.

18. Ibid., 38.

19. National Jewish Population Survey 2000–2001, http://www.ujc.org/page.html?ArticleID=46437.

20. Jewish Multiracial Network website, http://www.isabellafreedman.org/jmn/jmn_intro.shtml.

21. Yosef Abramowitz, "Going Where We're Growing: Including the Multiracial Jewish Community," http://www.caje.org/learn/a_abromowitz.htm.

22. For the Reform Movement, see Mark Washofsky, *Jewish Living: A Guide to Contemporary Reform Practice* (New York: UAHC Press, 2001), 142. For the Conservative movement, see Isaac Klein, *A Guide to Jewish Religious Practice* (New York: Jewish Theological Seminary of America, 1979), 437. For an Orthodox perspective, see Moshe Feinstein, *Igrot Moshe, Yoreh Deah* (2:174 sect. 4).

23. Data on remarriage rates is difficult to come by, but the trend is that divorce and remarriage are growing. See Barry A. Kosmin, Nava Lerer, and Egon Mayer, *Intermarriage, Divorce, and Remarriage among American Jews 1982–1987* (New York: North American Jewish Data Bank, 1989), http://www.jewishdatabank.org/Reports/Intermarriage_Divorce_Remarriage_Among_American_Jews_1989.pdf.

24. See, for example, Babylonian Talmud, *Bava Metzia* 39a, where *apotropos* refers to property, and *Pesachim* 49b, where the term refers to orphans.

25. Solomon B. Freehof, *Reform Responsa* (Cincinnati: Hebrew Union College Press, 1960), 32–34.

26. Some of these observations come from a beautiful article by a stepchild who became a stepparent, Jessica Klein Levenbrown, "Step by Step: A Stepchild Learns to Stepparent," http://www.chabad.org/theJewishWoman/article.asp?AID=377389.

27. For a more conventional telling of this story, see David Patterson, *The Greatest Jewish Stories Ever Told* (New York: Jonathan David Publishers, 1997), 301–02.

28. The quotation is in Sachs, *Good Enough Child*, 221, 253.

29. As taught by Rabbi M. Bruce Lustig of Washington Hebrew Congregation.

30. Ernest Kurtz and Katherine Ketchum, *The Spirituality of Imperfection* (New York: Bantam Books, 1992), 5.

Chapter 6: A Man within a Sacred Community

1. Barden, *Wrestling with Jacob and Esau*, 13.
2. David Murrow, *Why Men Hate Going to Church* (Nashville: Thomas Nelson, 2005), 53.
3. Ibid., 55.
4. Ibid., vii–viii.
5. Barden, *Wrestling with Jacob and Esau*, 11–13.
6. I do not agree with the theory proposed by Barden and others that the synagogue has gone so far as to become "feminized" by the increased presence of women. It is hard to see, from a liturgical point of view, how referring to God beyond gender as "the Eternal" instead of "the Lord" is feminizing. The liberal synagogue has not become a place of Goddess worship. The problem, rather, seems to be that men are abandoning a traditionally masculine role, not avoiding a feminine scene. It is true that women are taking on roles that were once considered masculine, while there is a limit to the extent to which men are willing to take on traditionally feminine roles. More women today are lawyers and doctors than a generation ago. Girls now play more competitive sports. Women now constitute about half of the purchasers at home improvement megastores (Pamela Sebastian Ridge, "Home Store Classes Encourage Women to Take Up Tools," *Wall Street Journal*, reprinted in *Anchorage Daily News*, April 1, 2002, sect. E, 8, as cited by Murrow *Why Men Hate Going to Church*, 110). On the other hand, even though men today are helping out more around the house and pushing strollers, they are not crocheting or playing mahjong. Men are not signing up to be kindergarten teachers. Boys have not joined ballet classes, certainly in anywhere near the same numbers as girls have signed up for soccer (Murrow, *Why Men Hate Going to Church*, 110).
7. Sandy Scott, "Women Volunteer at Higher Rates than Men Across U.S., New Federal Study Finds," Corporation for National & Community Service, June 13, 2006, http://www.nationalservice.org/about/newsroom/releases_detail.asp?tbl_pr_id=402.
8. Ibid.
9. Steven M. Cohen and Jack Wertheimer, "Whatever Happened to the Jewish People?" *Commentary*, June 2006, 33–37.
10. Scott, "Women Volunteer."
11. For a translation of this letter describing Maimonides' daily routine, see Jacob S. Minkin, *The World of Maimonides* (New York: Thomas Yoseloff, 1957), 154–55.
12. Moses Maimonides, *The Guide of the Perplexed*, trans. Shlomo Pines (Chicago: University of Chicago Press, 1963), I:72, 192.
13. Maimonides, *Guide*, II:11, 275.

14. Arthur Paul Boers, *Never Call Them Jerks: Healthy Responses to Difficult Behavior*, foreword by David W. Augsburger (Herndon, VA: The Alban Institute, 1999), vi.
15. Edwin H. Friedman, *Generation to Generation: Family Process in Church and Synagogue* (New York: Guilford Press, 1985), 27, 208–10.
16. Ibid., 229.
17. Cohen and Wertheimer, "Whatever Happened," 36.
18. The *machzor* or Jewish High Holy Day prayer book. See Stern, *Gates of Repentance*, 271–72.
19. This speech was delivered at Temple Sinai of Sharon, Massachusetts, and is used with the permission of his wife.

CHAPTER 7: THE *MITZVOT* OF MANHOOD

1. For another more traditional version of the story, see Patterson, *Greatest Jewish Stories*, 310.
2. This translation comes from Leonard Kravitz and Kerry M. Olitzky, *Shemonah Perakim: A Treatise on the Soul* (New York: UAHC Press, 1999), 33–35.
3. Ibid., 38.
4. Translation from Minkin, *World of Maimonides*, 382–83.
5. Bryan E. Robinson, *Chained to the Desk: A Guidebook for Workaholics, Their Partners and Children, and the Clinicians Who Treat Them* (New York: New York University Press, 2007).
6. Sid Kirchheimer, "Workaholism—the 'Respectable' Addiction," *WebMD*, 2000, http://www.webmd.com/mental-health/features/workaholism.
7. Workaholics Anonymous, http://www.workaholics-anonymous.org/index.html.
8. As taught to me by Rabbi Julie Schwartz.
9. Abraham Joshua Heschel, *The Sabbath: Its Meaning for Modern Man* (New York: Farrar, Straus, and Giroux, 1951), 14, based on *Zohar* I:75.
10. "Our God and God of Our Ancestors," attributed to the Baal Shem Tov as retold by Martin Buber, in Sidney Greenberg, *Likrat Shabbat* (Bridgeport, Conn.: Media Judaica, 1992), 106.
11. Antoine de Saint-Exupery, *Wind, Sand, and Stars* (San Diego, Calif.: Harcourt Brace & Company, 1967), 39.
12. James B. Twitchell, *Where Men Hide* (New York: Columbia University Press, 2006), 22.
13. Ibid., 241.
14. Ibid., 5.

Suggestions for Further Reading

Basic Jewish Sources

Benstein, Jeremy. *The Way Into Judaism and the Environment.* Woodstock, VT: Jewish Lights, 2008.

Cohen, Norman J. *The Way Into Torah.* Woodstock, VT: Jewish Lights, 2004.

Dorff, Elliot N. *The Way Into* Tikkun Olam *(Repairing the World).* Woodstock, VT: Jewish Lights, 2007.

Fishman, Sylvia Barack. *The Way Into the Varieties of Jewishness.* Woodstock, VT: Jewish Lights, 2008.

Gillman, Neil. *The Way Into Encountering God in Judaism.* Woodstock, VT: Jewish Lights, 2004.

Green, Arthur. *These Are the Words: A Vocabulary of Jewish Spiritual Life.* Woodstock, VT: Jewish Lights, 2000.

Hoffman, Lawrence A. *The Way Into Jewish Prayer.* Woodstock, VT: Jewish Lights, 2004.

Kravitz, Leonard, and Kerry M. Olitzky. Pirke Avot: *A Modern Commentary on Jewish Ethics.* New York: UAHC Press, 1993.

———. Shemonah Perakim: *A Treatise on the Soul.* New York: UAHC Press, 1999.

Kushner, Lawrence. *The Way Into Jewish Mystical Tradition.* Woodstock, VT: Jewish Lights, 2004.

Mack, Stan. *The Story of the Jews: A 4,000-Year Adventure—A Graphic History Book.* Woodstock, VT: Jewish Lights, 2001.

Matlins, Stuart M. *The Jewish Lights Spirituality Handbook: A Guide to Understanding, Exploring and Living a Spiritual Life.* Woodstock, VT: Jewish Lights, 2001.

Plaut,W. Gunther, and David E. S. Stein, eds. *The Torah: A Modern Commentary*, rev. ed. New York: Union for Reform Judaism, 2005.

Shapiro, Rami. *Ethics of the Sages:* Pirke Avot—*Annotated and Explained*. Woodstock, VT: Jewish Lights, 2006.

On Men and Judaism

Boyarin, Daniel. *Unheroic Conduct: The Rise of Heterosexuality and the Invention of the Jewish Man*. Berkeley: University of California Press, 1997.

Brod, Harry, ed. *A Mensch among Men: Explorations in Jewish Masculinity*. Freedom, CA: The Crossing Press, 1988.

Grishaver, Joel Lurie. *The Bonding of Isaac*. Los Angeles: Alef Design Group, 1997.

Pearl, Judea, and Ruth, eds. *I Am Jewish: Personal Reflections Inspired by the Last Words of Daniel Pearl*. Woodstock, VT: Jewish Lights, 2005.

Roth, Philip. *Portnoy's Complaint*. New York: Vintage International Vintage Books, 1967.

Salkin, Jeffrey K. *Searching for My Brothers: Jewish Men in a Gentile World*. New York: G. P. Putnam's Sons, 1999.

On Boys, Men, and Issues with Fathers

Moore, Robert, and Douglas Gillette. *King, Warrior, Magician, Lover: Rediscovering the Archetypes of the Mature Masculine*. San Francisco: HarperCollins, 1990.

Osherson, Samuel. *Finding Our Fathers*. New York: Contemporary Books, 2001.

Pittman, Frank. *Man Enough: Fathers, Sons, and the Search for Masculinity*. New York: Penguin Group, 1993.

Twitchell, James B. *Where Men Hide*. New York: Columbia University Press, 2006.

Viorst, Judith. *Necessary Losses: The Loves, Illusions, Dependencies, and Impossible Expectations That All of Us Have to Give Up in Order to Grow*. New York: Fawcett Columbine Books, 1986.

On Marriage and Relationships with Women

Fuchs-Kreimer, Nancy. *Judaism for Two: A Spiritual Guide for Strengthening and Celebrating Your Loving Relationship*. Woodstock, VT: Jewish Lights, 2005.

Rhoads, Steven E. *Taking Sex Differences Seriously*. San Francisco: Encounter Books, 2004.

Wallerstein, Judith S., and Sandra Blakeslee. *The Good Marriage: How & Why Love Lasts*. New York: Warner Books, 1995.

On Parenting

Doades, Joanne. *Parenting Jewish Teens: A Guide for the Perplexed*. Woodstock, VT: Jewish Lights, 2006.

Fuchs-Kreimer, Nancy. *Parenting as a Spiritual Journey: Deepening Ordinary and Extraordinary Events into Sacred Occasions*. Woodstock, VT: Jewish Lights, 1998.

Mogel, Wendy. *The Blessing of a Skinned Knee*. New York: Penguin Books, 2001.

Sachs, Brad E. *Blind Date: Poems of Expectant Fatherhood*. Baltimore: Chestnut Hills Press, 1992.

———. *The Good Enough Child: How to Have an Imperfect Family and Be Perfectly Satisfied*. New York: HarperCollins, 2001.

On Workaholism

Robinson, Bryan E. *Chained to the Desk: A Guidebook for Workaholics, Their Partners and Children, and the Clinicians Who Treat Them*. New York: New York University Press, 2007.

Bar/Bat Mitzvah

The JGirl's Guide: The Young Jewish Woman's Handbook for Coming of Age
By Penina Adelman, Ali Feldman, and Shulamit Reinharz
This inspirational, interactive guidebook helps pre-teen Jewish girls address the many issues surrounding coming of age.   6 x 9, 240 pp, Quality PB, 978-1-58023-215-9 **$14.99**

Also Available: **The JGirl's Teacher's and Parent's Guide**
8½ x 11, 56 pp, PB, 978-1-58023-225-8 **$8.99**

Bar/Bat Mitzvah Basics: A Practical Family Guide to Coming of Age Together
Edited by Cantor Helen Leneman   6 x 9, 240 pp, Quality PB, 978-1-58023-151-0 **$18.95**

The Bar/Bat Mitzvah Memory Book, 2nd Edition: An Album for Treasuring the Spiritual Celebration *By Rabbi Jeffrey K. Salkin and Nina Salkin*
8 x 10, 48 pp, Deluxe HC, 2-color text, ribbon marker, 978-1-58023-263-0 **$19.99**

For Kids—Putting God on Your Guest List, 2nd Edition: How to Claim the Spiritual Meaning of Your Bar or Bat Mitzvah *By Rabbi Jeffrey K. Salkin*
6 x 9, 144 pp, Quality PB, 978-1-58023-308-8 **$15.99** *For ages 11–13*

Putting God on the Guest List, 3rd Edition: How to Reclaim the Spiritual Meaning of Your Child's Bar or Bat Mitzvah *By Rabbi Jeffrey K. Salkin*
6 x 9, 224 pp, Quality PB, 978-1-58023-222-7 **$16.99**; HC, 978-1-58023-260-9 **$24.99**

Also Available: **Putting God on the Guest List Teacher's Guide**
8½ x 11, 48 pp, PB, 978-1-58023-226-5 **$8.99**

Tough Questions Jews Ask: A Young Adult's Guide to Building a Jewish Life
By Rabbi Edward Feinstein 6 x 9, 160 pp, Quality PB, 978-1-58023-139-8 **$14.99** *For ages 12 & up*

Also Available: **Tough Questions Jews Ask Teacher's Guide**
8½ x 11, 72 pp, PB, 978-1-58023-187-9 **$8.95**

Bible Study/Midrash

Abraham's Bind & Other Bible Tales of Trickery, Folly, Mercy and Love *By Michael J. Caduto*
Re-imagines many biblical characters, retelling their stories.
6 x 9, 224 pp, HC, 978-1-59473-186-0 **$19.99** *(A SkyLight Paths book)*

Ancient Secrets: Using the Stories of the Bible to Improve Our Everyday Lives
By Rabbi Levi Meier, PhD 5½ x 8½, 288 pp, Quality PB, 978-1-58023-064-3 **$16.95**

The Genesis of Leadership: What the Bible Teaches Us about Vision, Values and Leading Change *By Rabbi Nathan Laufer; Foreword by Senator Joseph I. Lieberman*
Unlike other books on leadership, this one is rooted in the stories of the Bible.
6 x 9, 288 pp, Quality PB, 978-1-58023-352-1 **$18.99**; HC, 978-1-58023-241-8 **$24.99**

Hineini in Our Lives: Learning How to Respond to Others through 14 Biblical Texts and Personal Stories *By Norman J. Cohen* 6 x 9, 240 pp, Quality PB, 978-1-58023-274-6 **$16.99**

Moses and the Journey to Leadership: Timeless Lessons of Effective Management from the Bible and Today's Leaders *By Dr. Norman J. Cohen*
6 x 9, 240 pp, Quality PB, 978-1-58023-351-4 **$18.99**; HC, 978-1-58023-227-2 **$21.99**

Self, Struggle & Change: Family Conflict Stories in Genesis and Their Healing Insights for Our Lives *By Norman J. Cohen* 6 x 9, 224 pp, Quality PB, 978-1-879045-66-8 **$18.99**

The Triumph of Eve & Other Subversive Bible Tales *By Matt Biers-Ariel*
5½ x 8½, 192 pp, Quality PB, 978-1-59473-176-1 **$14.99**; HC, 978-1-59473-040-5 **$19.99**
(A SkyLight Paths book)

The Wisdom of Judaism: An Introduction to the Values of the Talmud
By Rabbi Dov Peretz Elkins
Explores the essence of Judaism.   6 x 9, 192 pp, Quality PB, 978-1-58023-327-9 **$16.99**

Also Available: **The Wisdom of Judaism Teacher's Guide**
8½ x 11, 18 pp, PB, 978-1-58023-350-7 **$8.99**

Or phone, fax, mail or e-mail to: **JEWISH LIGHTS** Publishing
Sunset Farm Offices, Route 4 • P.O. Box 237 • Woodstock, Vermont 05091
Tel: (802) 457-4000 • Fax: (802) 457-4004 • www.jewishlights.com

Credit card orders: (800) 962-4544 (8:30AM–5:30PM ET Monday–Friday)
Generous discounts on quantity orders. SATISFACTION GUARANTEED. Prices subject to change.

Congregation Resources

The Art of Public Prayer, 2nd Edition: Not for Clergy Only *By Lawrence A. Hoffman*
6 x 9, 272 pp, Quality PB, 978-1-893361-06-5 **$19.99** *(A SkyLight Paths book)*

Becoming a Congregation of Learners: Learning as a Key to Revitalizing
Congregational Life *By Isa Aron, PhD; Foreword by Rabbi Lawrence A. Hoffman*
6 x 9, 304 pp, Quality PB, 978-1-58023-089-6 **$19.95**

Finding a Spiritual Home: How a New Generation of Jews Can Transform the
American Synagogue *By Rabbi Sidney Schwarz*
6 x 9, 352 pp, Quality PB, 978-1-58023-185-5 **$19.95**

Jewish Pastoral Care, 2nd Edition: A Practical Handbook from Traditional &
Contemporary Sources *Edited by Rabbi Dayle A. Friedman*
6 x 9, 528 pp, HC, 978-1-58023-221-0 **$40.00**

Jewish Spiritual Direction: An Innovative Guide from Traditional and Contemporary
Sources *Edited by Rabbi Howard A. Addison and Barbara Eve Breitman*
6 x 9, 368 pp, HC, 978-1-58023-230-2 **$30.00**

The Self-Renewing Congregation: Organizational Strategies for Revitalizing
Congregational Life *By Isa Aron, PhD; Foreword by Dr. Ron Wolfson*
6 x 9, 304 pp, Quality PB, 978-1-58023-166-4 **$19.95**

Spiritual Community: The Power to Restore Hope, Commitment and Joy
By Rabbi David A. Teutsch, PhD 5½ x 8½, 144 pp, HC, 978-1-58023-270-8 **$19.99**

The Spirituality of Welcoming: How to Transform Your Congregation into a
Sacred Community *By Dr. Ron Wolfson* 6 x 9, 224 pp, Quality PB, 978-1-58023-244-9 **$19.99**

Rethinking Synagogues: A New Vocabulary for Congregational Life
By Rabbi Lawrence A. Hoffman 6 x 9, 240 pp, Quality PB, 978-1-58023-248-7 **$19.99**

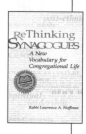

Children's Books

What You Will See Inside a Synagogue
By Rabbi Lawrence A. Hoffman and Dr. Ron Wolfson; Full-color photos by Bill Aron
A colorful, fun-to-read introduction that explains the ways and whys of Jewish
worship and religious life. 8½ x 10½, 32 pp, Full-color photos, Quality PB, 978-1-59473-256-0 **$8.99**
For ages 6 & up (A SkyLight Paths book)

The Kids' Fun Book of Jewish Time
By Emily Sper 9 x 7½, 24 pp, Full-color illus., HC, 978-1-58023-311-8 **$16.99**

In God's Hands
By Lawrence Kushner and Gary Schmidt 9 x 12, 32 pp, HC, 978-1-58023-224-1 **$16.99**

Because Nothing Looks Like God
By Lawrence and Karen Kushner
Introduces children to the possibilities of spiritual life.
11 x 8½, 32 pp, Full-color illus., HC, 978-1-58023-092-6 **$17.99** *For ages 4 & up*

Also Available: **Because Nothing Looks Like God Teacher's Guide**
8½ x 11, 22 pp, PB, 978-1-58023-140-4 **$6.95** *For ages 5–8*

Board Book Companions to *Because Nothing Looks Like God*
5 x 5, 24 pp, Full-color illus., SkyLight Paths Board Books *For ages 0–4*

What Does God Look Like? 978-1-893361-23-2 **$7.99**

How Does God Make Things Happen? 978-1-893361-24-9 **$7.95**

Where Is God? 978-1-893361-17-1 **$7.99**

The Book of Miracles: A Young Person's Guide to Jewish Spiritual Awareness
By Lawrence Kushner. All-new illustrations by the author
6 x 9, 96 pp, 2-color illus., HC, 978-1-879045-78-1 **$16.95** *For ages 9 and up*

In Our Image: God's First Creatures
By Nancy Sohn Swartz 9 x 12, 32 pp, Full-color illus., HC, 978-1-879045-99-6 **$16.95** *For ages 4 & up*

Also Available as a Board Book: **How Did the Animals Help God?**
5 x 5, 24 pp, Board, Full-color illus., 978-1-59473-044-3 **$7.99** *For ages 0–4 (A SkyLight Paths book)*

What Makes Someone a Jew?
By Lauren Seidman
Reflects the changing face of American Judaism.
10 x 8½, 32 pp, Full-color photos, Quality PB Original, 978-1-58023-321-7 **$8.99** *For ages 3–6*

Holidays/Holy Days

Rosh Hashanah Readings: Inspiration, Information and Contemplation
Yom Kippur Readings: Inspiration, Information and Contemplation
Edited by Rabbi Dov Peretz Elkins with Section Introductions from Arthur Green's These Are the Words
An extraordinary collection of readings, prayers and insights that enable the modern worshiper to enter into the spirit of the High Holy Days in a personal and powerful way, permitting the meaning of the Jewish New Year to enter the heart.
RHR: 6 x 9, 400 pp, HC, 978-1-58023-239-5 **$24.99**
YKR: 6 x 9, 368 pp, HC, 978-1-58023-271-5 **$24.99**

Jewish Holidays: A Brief Introduction for Christians
By Rabbi Kerry M. Olitzky and Rabbi Daniel Judson
5½ x 8½, 144 pp, Quality PB, 978-1-58023-302-6 **$16.99**

Reclaiming Judaism as a Spiritual Practice: Holy Days and Shabbat
By Rabbi Goldie Milgram
7 x 9, 272 pp, Quality PB, 978-1-58023-205-0 **$19.99**

7th Heaven: Celebrating Shabbat with Rebbe Nachman of Breslov
By Moshe Mykoff with the Breslov Research Institute
5⅛ x 8¼, 224 pp, Deluxe PB w/flaps, 978-1-58023-175-6 **$18.95**

Shabbat, 2nd Edition: The Family Guide to Preparing for and Celebrating the Sabbath
By Dr. Ron Wolfson 7 x 9, 320 pp, illus., Quality PB, 978-1-58023-164-0 **$19.99**

Hanukkah, 2nd Edition: The Family Guide to Spiritual Celebration
By Dr. Ron Wolfson. Edited by Joel Lurie Grishaver.
7 x 9, 240 pp, illus., Quality PB, 978-1-58023-122-0 **$18.95**

The Jewish Family Fun Book, 2nd Edition: Holiday Projects, Everyday Activities, and Travel Ideas with Jewish Themes *By Danielle Dardashti and Roni Sarig. Illus. by Avi Katz.*
6 x 9, 304 pp, 70+ b/w illus. & diagrams, Quality PB, 978-1-58023-333-0 **$18.99**

The Jewish Lights Book of Fun Classroom Activities: Simple and Seasonal Projects for Teachers and Students *By Danielle Dardashti and Roni Sarig*
6 x 9, 240 pp, Quality PB, 978-1-58023-206-7 **$19.99**

Passover

My People's Passover Haggadah
Traditional Texts, Modern Commentaries
Edited by Rabbi Lawrence A. Hoffman, PhD, and David Arnow, PhD
A diverse and exciting collection of commentaries on the traditional Passover Haggadah—in two volumes!
Vol. 1: 7 x 10, 304 pp, HC, 978-1-58023-354-5 **$24.99**
Vol. 2: 7 x 10, 320 pp, HC, 978-1-58023-346-0 **$24.99**

Leading the Passover Journey
The Seder's Meaning Revealed, the Haggadah's Story Retold
By Rabbi Nathan Laufer
Uncovers the hidden meaning of the Seder's rituals and customs.
6 x 9, 224 pp, HC, 978-1-58023-211-1 **$24.99**

The Women's Passover Companion: Women's Reflections on the Festival of Freedom
Edited by Rabbi Sharon Cohen Anisfeld, Tara Mohr, and Catherine Spector
6 x 9, 352 pp, Quality PB, 978-1-58023-231-9 **$19.99**

The Women's Seder Sourcebook: Rituals & Readings for Use at the Passover Seder
Edited by Rabbi Sharon Cohen Anisfeld, Tara Mohr, and Catherine Spector
6 x 9, 384 pp, Quality PB, 978-1-58023-232-6 **$19.99**

Creating Lively Passover Seders: A Sourcebook of Engaging Tales, Texts & Activities
By David Arnow, PhD 7 x 9, 416 pp, Quality PB, 978-1-58023-184-8 **$24.99**

Passover, 2nd Edition: The Family Guide to Spiritual Celebration
By Dr. Ron Wolfson with Joel Lurie Grishaver 7 x 9, 352 pp, Quality PB, 978-1-58023-174-9 **$19.95**

Life Cycle
Marriage / Parenting / Family / Aging

The New Jewish Baby Album: Creating and Celebrating the Beginning of a Spiritual Life—A Jewish Lights Companion
By the Editors at Jewish Lights. Foreword by Anita Diamant. Preface by Rabbi Sandy Eisenberg Sasso.
A spiritual keepsake that will be treasured for generations. More than just a memory book, *shows you how—and why it's important*—to create a Jewish home and a Jewish life. 8 x 10, 64 pp, Deluxe Padded HC, Full-color illus., 978-1-58023-138-1 **$19.95**

The Jewish Pregnancy Book: A Resource for the Soul, Body & Mind during Pregnancy, Birth & the First Three Months
By Sandy Falk, MD, and Rabbi Daniel Judson, with Steven A. Rapp
Includes medical information, prayers and rituals for each stage of pregnancy, from a liberal Jewish perspective. 7 x 10, 208 pp, Quality PB, b/w photos, 978-1-58023-178-7 **$16.95**

Celebrating Your New Jewish Daughter: Creating Jewish Ways to Welcome Baby Girls into the Covenant—New and Traditional Ceremonies *By Debra Nussbaum Cohen; Foreword by Rabbi Sandy Eisenberg Sasso* 6 x 9, 272 pp, Quality PB, 978-1-58023-090-2 **$18.95**

The New Jewish Baby Book, 2nd Edition: Names, Ceremonies & Customs—A Guide for Today's Families *By Anita Diamant* 6 x 9, 336 pp, Quality PB, 978-1-58023-251-7 **$19.99**

Parenting as a Spiritual Journey: Deepening Ordinary and Extraordinary Events into Sacred Occasions *By Rabbi Nancy Fuchs-Kreimer*
6 x 9, 224 pp, Quality PB, 978-1-58023-016-2 **$16.95**

Parenting Jewish Teens: A Guide for the Perplexed
By Joanne Doades
Explores the questions and issues that shape the world in which today's Jewish teenagers live.
6 x 9, 200 pp, Quality PB, 978-1-58023-305-7 **$16.99**

Judaism for Two: A Spiritual Guide for Strengthening and Celebrating Your Loving Relationship *By Rabbi Nancy Fuchs-Kreimer and Rabbi Nancy H. Wiener; Foreword by Rabbi Elliot N. Dorff* Addresses the ways Jewish teachings can enhance and strengthen committed relationships. 6 x 9, 224 pp, Quality PB, 978-1-58023-254-8 **$16.99**

Embracing the Covenant: Converts to Judaism Talk About Why & How
By Rabbi Allan Berkowitz and Patti Moskovitz 6 x 9, 192 pp, Quality PB, 978-1-879045-50-7 **$16.95**

The Guide to Jewish Interfaith Family Life: An InterfaithFamily.com Handbook
Edited by Ronnie Friedland and Edmund Case 6 x 9, 384 pp, Quality PB, 978-1-58023-153-4 **$18.95**

Introducing My Faith and My Community
The Jewish Outreach Institute Guide for the Christian in a Jewish Interfaith Relationship
By Rabbi Kerry M. Olitzky 6 x 9, 176 pp, Quality PB, 978-1-58023-192-3 **$16.99**

Making a Successful Jewish Interfaith Marriage: The Jewish Outreach Institute Guide to Opportunities, Challenges and Resources *By Rabbi Kerry M. Olitzky with Joan Peterson Littman*
6 x 9, 176 pp, Quality PB, 978-1-58023-170-1 **$16.95**

The Creative Jewish Wedding Book: A Hands-On Guide to New & Old Traditions, Ceremonies & Celebrations *By Gabrielle Kaplan-Mayer*
9 x 9, 288 pp, b/w photos, Quality PB, 978-1-58023-194-7 **$19.99**

Divorce Is a Mitzvah: A Practical Guide to Finding Wholeness and Holiness When Your Marriage Dies *By Rabbi Perry Netter; Afterword by Rabbi Laura Geller.*
6 x 9, 224 pp, Quality PB, 978-1-58023-172-5 **$16.95**

A Heart of Wisdom: Making the Jewish Journey from Midlife through the Elder Years
Edited by Susan Berrin; Foreword by Harold Kushner
6 x 9, 384 pp, Quality PB, 978-1-58023-051-3 **$18.95**

So That Your Values Live On: Ethical Wills and How to Prepare Them
Edited by Jack Riemer and Nathaniel Stampfer
6 x 9, 272 pp, Quality PB, 978-1-879045-34-7 **$18.99**

Spirituality/Lawrence Kushner

Filling Words with Light: Hasidic and Mystical Reflections on Jewish Prayer
By Lawrence Kushner and Nehemia Polen
5½ x 8½, 176 pp, Quality PB, 978-1-58023-238-8 **$16.99**; HC, 978-1-58023-216-6 **$21.99**

The Book of Letters: A Mystical Hebrew Alphabet
Popular HC Edition, 6 x 9, 80 pp, 2-color text, 978-1-879045-00-2 **$24.95**
Collector's Limited Edition, 9 x 12, 80 pp, gold foil embossed pages, w/limited edition silkscreened
print, 978-1-879045-04-0 **$349.00**

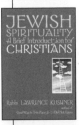

The Book of Miracles: A Young Person's Guide to Jewish Spiritual Awareness
6 x 9, 96 pp, 2-color illus., HC, 978-1-879045-78-1 **$16.95** *For ages 9 and up*

The Book of Words: Talking Spiritual Life, Living Spiritual Talk
6 x 9, 160 pp, Quality PB, 978-1-58023-020-9 **$16.95**

Eyes Remade for Wonder: A Lawrence Kushner Reader *Introduction by Thomas Moore*
6 x 9, 240 pp, Quality PB, 978-1-58023-042-1 **$18.95**

God Was in This Place & I, i Did Not Know: Finding Self, Spirituality and
Ultimate Meaning 6 x 9, 192 pp, Quality PB, 978-1-879045-33-0 **$16.95**

Honey from the Rock: An Introduction to Jewish Mysticism
6 x 9, 176 pp, Quality PB, 978-1-58023-073-5 **$16.95**

Invisible Lines of Connection: Sacred Stories of the Ordinary
5½ x 8½, 160 pp, Quality PB, 978-1-879045-98-9 **$15.95**

Jewish Spirituality—A Brief Introduction for Christians
5½ x 8½, 112 pp, Quality PB, 978-1-58023-150-3 **$12.95**

The River of Light: Jewish Mystical Awareness
6 x 9, 192 pp, Quality PB, 978-1-58023-096-4 **$16.95**

The Way Into Jewish Mystical Tradition
6 x 9, 224 pp, Quality PB, 978-1-58023-200-5 **$18.99**; HC, 978-1-58023-029-2 **$21.95**

Spirituality/Prayer

My People's Passover Haggadah: Traditional Texts, Modern Commentaries
Edited by Rabbi Lawrence A. Hoffman, PhD, and David Arnow, PhD Diverse commentaries
on the traditional Passover Haggadah—in two volumes! Vol. 1: 7 x 10, 304 pp, HC
978-1-58023-354-5 **$24.99** Vol. 2: 7 x 10, 320 pp, HC, 978-1-58023-346-0 **$24.99**

Witnesses to the One: The Spiritual History of the *Sh'ma By Rabbi Joseph B.
Meszler; Foreword by Rabbi Elyse Goldstein* 6 x 9, 176 pp, HC, 978-1-58023-309-5 **$19.99**

My People's Prayer Book Series

Traditional Prayers, Modern Commentaries *Edited by Rabbi Lawrence A. Hoffman*
Provides diverse and exciting commentary to the traditional liturgy, helping modern
men and women find new wisdom in Jewish prayer, and bring liturgy into their lives.
Each book includes Hebrew text, modern translation, and commentaries from all
perspectives of the Jewish world.

Vol. 1—The *Sh'ma* and Its Blessings
7 x 10, 168 pp, HC, 978-1-879045-79-8 **$24.99**
Vol. 2—The *Amidah*
7 x 10, 240 pp, HC, 978-1-879045-80-4 **$24.95**
Vol. 3—*P'sukei D'zimrah* (Morning Psalms)
7 x 10, 240 pp, HC, 978-1-879045-81-1 **$24.95**
Vol. 4—*Seder K'riat Hatorah* (The Torah Service)
7 x 10, 264 pp, HC, 978-1-879045-82-8 **$23.95**
Vol. 5—*Birkhot Hashachar* (Morning Blessings)
7 x 10, 240 pp, HC, 978-1-879045-83-5 **$24.95**
Vol. 6—*Tachanun* and Concluding Prayers
7 x 10, 240 pp, HC, 978-1-879045-84-2 **$24.95**
Vol. 7—Shabbat at Home
7 x 10, 240 pp, HC, 978-1-879045-85-9 **$24.95**
Vol. 8—*Kabbalat Shabbat* (Welcoming Shabbat in the Synagogue)
7 x 10, 240 pp, HC, 978-1-58023-121-3 **$24.99**
Vol. 9—Welcoming the Night: *Minchah* and *Ma'ariv* (Afternoon and
Evening Prayer) 7 x 10, 272 pp, HC, 978-1-58023-262-3 **$24.99**
Vol. 10—Shabbat Morning: *Shacharit* and *Musaf* (Morning and
Additional Services) 7 x 10, 240 pp, HC, 978-1-58023-240-1 **$24.99**

Spirituality

Journeys to a Jewish Life: Inspiring Stories from the Spiritual Journeys of American Jews *By Paula Amann*
Examines the soul treks of Jews lost and found. 6 x 9, 208 pp, HC, 978-1-58023-317-0 **$19.99**

The Adventures of Rabbi Harvey: A Graphic Novel of Jewish Wisdom and Wit in the Wild West *By Steve Sheinkin*
Jewish and American folktales combine in this witty and original graphic novel collection. Creatively retold and set on the western frontier of the 1870s.
6 x 9, 144 pp, Full-color illus., Quality PB, 978-1-58023-310-1 **$16.99**
Also Available: **The Adventures of Rabbi Harvey Teacher's Guide**
8½ x 11, 32 pp, PB, 978-1-58023-326-2 **$8.99**

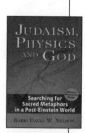

Ethics of the Sages: Pirke Avot—Annotated & Explained
Translation and Annotation by Rabbi Rami Shapiro
5½ x 8½, 192 pp, Quality PB, 978-1-59473-207-2 **$16.99** *(A SkyLight Paths book)*

A Book of Life: Embracing Judaism as a Spiritual Practice
By Michael Strassfeld 6 x 9, 528 pp, Quality PB, 978-1-58023-247-0 **$19.99**

Meaning and Mitzvah: Daily Practices for Reclaiming Judaism through Prayer, God, Torah, Hebrew, Mitzvot and Peoplehood *By Rabbi Goldie Milgram*
7 x 9, 336 pp, Quality PB, 978-1-58023-256-2 **$19.99**

The Soul of the Story: Meetings with Remarkable People
By Rabbi David Zeller 6 x 9, 288 pp, HC, 978-1-58023-272-2 **$21.99**

Aleph-Bet Yoga: Embodying the Hebrew Letters for Physical and Spiritual Well-Being
By Steven A. Rapp. Foreword by Tamar Frankiel, PhD and Judy Greenfeld. Preface by Hart Lazer.
7 x 10, 128 pp, b/w photos, Quality PB, Layflat binding, 978-1-58023-162-6 **$16.95**

Does the Soul Survive? A Jewish Journey to Belief in Afterlife, Past Lives & Living with Purpose *By Rabbi Elie Kaplan Spitz; Foreword by Brian L. Weiss, MD*
6 x 9, 288 pp, Quality PB, 978-1-58023-165-7 **$16.99**

First Steps to a New Jewish Spirit: Reb Zalman's Guide to Recapturing the Intimacy & Ecstasy in Your Relationship with God *By Rabbi Zalman M. Schachter-Shalomi with Donald Gropman* 6 x 9, 144 pp, Quality PB, 978-1-58023-182-4 **$16.95**

God in Our Relationships: Spirituality between People from the Teachings of Martin Buber *By Rabbi Dennis S. Ross* 5½ x 8½, 160 pp, Quality PB, 978-1-58023-147-3 **$16.95**

Judaism, Physics and God: Searching for Sacred Metaphors in a Post-Einstein World
By Rabbi David W. Nelson 6 x 9, 368 pp, Quality PB, inc. reader's discussion guide, 978-1-58023-306-4 **$18.99**;
HC, 352 pp, 978-1-58023-252-4 **$24.99**

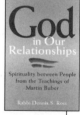

The Jewish Lights Spirituality Handbook: A Guide to Understanding, Exploring & Living a Spiritual Life *Edited by Stuart M. Matlins*
What exactly is "Jewish" about spirituality? How do I make it a part of my life? Fifty of today's foremost spiritual leaders share their ideas and experience with us.
6 x 9, 456 pp, Quality PB, 978-1-58023-093-3 **$19.99**

Bringing the Psalms to Life: How to Understand and Use the Book of Psalms
By Daniel F. Polish 6 x 9, 208 pp, Quality PB, 978-1-58023-157-2 **$16.95**;
HC, 978-1-58023-077-3 **$21.95**

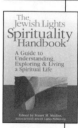

God & the Big Bang: Discovering Harmony between Science & Spirituality
By Daniel C. Matt 6 x 9, 216 pp, Quality PB, 978-1-879045-89-7 **$16.99**

Minding the Temple of the Soul: Balancing Body, Mind, and Spirit through Traditional Jewish Prayer, Movement, and Meditation *By Tamar Frankiel, PhD, and Judy Greenfeld*
7 x 10, 184 pp, illus., Quality PB, 978-1-879045-64-4 **$16.95**
Audiotape of the Blessings and Meditations: 60 min. **$9.95**
Videotape of the Movements and Meditations: 46 min. **$20.00**

One God Clapping: The Spiritual Path of a Zen Rabbi *By Alan Lew with Sherril Jaffe*
5½ x 8½, 336 pp, Quality PB, 978-1-58023-115-2 **$16.95**

There Is No Messiah ... and You're It: The Stunning Transformation of Judaism's Most Provocative Idea *By Rabbi Robert N. Levine, DD*
6 x 9, 192 pp, Quality PB, 978-1-58023-255-5 **$16.99**

These Are the Words: A Vocabulary of Jewish Spiritual Life
By Arthur Green 6 x 9, 304 pp, Quality PB, 978-1-58023-107-7 **$18.95**

About Jewish Lights

People of all faiths and backgrounds yearn for books that attract, engage, educate, and spiritually inspire.

Our principal goal is to stimulate thought and help all people learn about who the Jewish People are, where they come from, and what the future can be made to hold. While people of our diverse Jewish heritage are the primary audience, our books speak to people in the Christian world as well and will broaden their understanding of Judaism and the roots of their own faith.

We bring to you authors who are at the forefront of spiritual thought and experience. While each has something different to say, they all say it in a voice that you can hear.

Our books are designed to welcome you and then to engage, stimulate, and inspire. We judge our success not only by whether or not our books are beautiful and commercially successful, but by whether or not they make a difference in your life.

For your information and convenience, at the back of this book we have provided a list of other Jewish Lights books you might find interesting and useful. They cover all the categories of your life:

Bar/Bat Mitzvah	Life Cycle
Bible Study / Midrash	Meditation
Children's Books	Parenting
Congregation Resources	Prayer
Current Events / History	Ritual / Sacred Practice
Ecology/ Environment	Spirituality
Fiction: Mystery, Science Fiction	Theology / Philosophy
Grief / Healing	Travel
Holidays / Holy Days	12-Step
Inspiration	Women's Interest
Kabbalah / Mysticism / Enneagram	

Stuart M. Matlins

Stuart M. Matlins, Publisher

Or phone, fax, mail or e-mail to: **JEWISH LIGHTS Publishing**
Sunset Farm Offices, Route 4 • P.O. Box 237 • Woodstock, Vermont 05091
Tel: (802) 457-4000 • Fax: (802) 457-4004 • www.jewishlights.com
Credit card orders: **(800) 962-4544** (8:30AM–5:30PM ET Monday–Friday)
Generous discounts on quantity orders. SATISFACTION GUARANTEED. Prices subject to change.

For more information about each book, visit our website at www.jewishlights.com